A Story of Love, Loss, and Love Again

A Widow,
a Chihuahua,
and
Harry Truman

Mary Beth Crain

HarperSanFrancisco
A Division of HarperCollins*Publishers*

HarperCollins books may be purchased for educational, business, or sales promotional use. For information please write: Special Markets Department, HarperCollins Publishers Inc., 10 East 53rd Street, New York, NY 10022.

HarperCollins Web site: http://www.harpercollins.com

HarperCollins®, ☙®, and HarperSanFrancisco™ are trademarks of HarperCollins Publishers Inc.

FIRST EDITION

Library of Congress Cataloging-in-Publication Data
Crain, Mary Beth.
   A widow, a chihuahua, and Harry Truman : a story of love, loss, and love again / Mary Beth Crain. — 1st ed.
      p.   cm.
   ISBN 0–06–251672–8 (cloth)
   ISBN 0–06–251673–6 (pbk.)
      1. Chihuahua (Dog breed)—California—Los Angeles—Biography.   2. Crain, Mary Beth.   3. Women dog owners—California—Los Angeles—Biography.
   4. Widows—California—Los Angeles—Biography.   5. Human-animal relationships.   I. Title.
SF429.C45 C73 2000
636.76—dc21   00–027732

00 01 02 03 04 ❖RRD(H) 10 9 8 7 6 5 4 3 2 1

To Adam and St. Francis of Assisi,

both of whom loved all creatures,

great and small

Contents

If you want a friend in Washington, get a dog.

—*Harry S. Truman*

How often we hear the remark, "Yes, I like dogs," hastily followed by "*Big* dogs, that is!" thus dismissing little dogs as being beneath notice. I don't bother to argue but can't help thinking each time, "Oh, you don't know what you're missing!"

I have one of each—a golden retriever and a shih tzu. Personally, I love 'em all, whatever size. (I used to say "Anything with a leg on each corner," but I've come to know some wonderful three-legged cancer survivors.) However, there's something about the little ones that has always reduced me to jelly. First of all, they're so totally oblivious to the fact that they're undersize; in addition, they're so delightfully portable.

A word of warning: set some ground rules going in or you're lost. That very portability makes it too easy simply to pick them up and put them where you want them to be, rather than teach them what they should do. (And *not* do!) Once they discover that they can get away with misbehaving by turning on the adorableness, the balance of power changes hands forever.

Want a classic example? Meet Truman. Mary Beth Crain lost her heart to something that weighed much less than her purse. Our author did all the things I've preached against for years. She bought Truman on impulse—in a pet shop; she neglected to set basic guidelines when she brought him home; she gave him everything but the keys to the car (and consequently was reduced to being epsilon to his alpha). Small as he is, of course, all Truman did for her in return was lift her out of a very bad time in her life, put the sun back in the sky, and restore her sense of humor. He's made such a place for himself that I'll be surprised if he doesn't demand author credit.

Shows how much I know with all my preaching!

May I make one personal request? The next time you're tempted to take a small dog less than seriously, think of Truman and the way he patched up the hole in Mary Beth's life. Or, for that matter, give a thought to all the little guys and girls who have helped me over the hard places throughout my life, making me laugh, or drying my tears—Panda, Timothy, Cricket, Bandit, Nicky, Bootie, Willie, Emma, Binky, Simba—the list goes on.

Here's to you, Truman. Ever thought of running for president?

Love,
Betty White

Acknowledgments

This book has been a labor of love in more ways than one. I loved writing it and paying tribute to the man I loved, as well as the man whose presidency I wish I'd been old enough to remember. It has also reminded me many times over of the number of people who have loved and supported me, and whom I would like to take this opportunity to thank:

Sister Janet Harris, the world's best friend and neighbor, who listened to every chapter hot out of the printer and cheered me on every step of the way, and who has babysat Truman above and beyond the call of duty.

Sant Kaur Khalsa, Truman's number-two mom, the world's best dog-sitter and a wonderful friend, who has put up with Truman's shenanigans with long-suffering patience and whose own dog, Missy, has been a stellar example of canine propriety.

Dave Gersten, the world's best twin brother and my harshest critic—when you liked a chapter I knew it was good—and his wife, Deb, for always being there to listen and help me through the bad and good times.

Joanna Rice, my dear pal and fellow chihuahua mom, who has provided Truman with many of the nicest additions to his wardrobe, and me with a wonderful new friendship—and

Todd, her fantastic husband, and Buddy Boy, her brilliant little man.

Terry Taylor—what a support you've been, always there to listen to these chapters and remind me that this book was what I was supposed to be doing with my life, always there with invaluable suggestions and insight as a fellow writer, artist, and spiritual seeker. I am blessed by your friendship!

Claire Bucalos, my wonderful cousin, for all your love and support through the years. Where would I have been without your advice on the book and on the fine (if harrowing) art of puppy-raising? And a special acknowledgment to your fine specimens of golden retrieverhood, Cider Marie and Casey Francis, for providing Truman with good role models.

Christine Shields, my sister-in-law, whose enjoyment of the manuscript and unfailing encouragement gave me confidence in the project, and whose love for her brother Adam and help to me after his death will never be forgotten.

Those other Birds, Scarlet O'Conner and Veronica McClure, for their love, friendship, and bond of sisterhood, which have meant so much to me.

Ellen Krout-Hasegawa, who stoically refused to let me procrastinate on this project and whose loving support and badgering helped me to finish it.

Adam's children—Mike, Tim, Sara, and Jenny—and his daughters-in-law—Sandy and Kathy—for the many moments of joy and pride they gave Adam, and for their help and love during his illness and death.

My brilliant editor, Liz Perle, without whose faith, commitment, and vision this book might never have been, and whose insight and direction made it into something far better than it might have been.

Liz's assistant editor, David Hennessy, who turned out to be a damn good editor, production manager, and all-round support, even if he was only twenty-nine.

My incredible friend of thirty years, Steven Vance—your unfailing love, empathy, humor, and encouragement before, during, and after Adam's death, and throughout the whole arduous process of getting this book written and sold, has been a constant reminder of the meaning of true friendship.

Casey Cohen, who passed away while this book was in production, and whose courage, wisdom, and insights about Harry Truman were invaluable to me.

My agent, Loretta Barrett, for her belief in me, her support of this project, and her valued friendship, which have made her far more than just an agent in my life.

My mom, Hazel Gersten, for encouraging a love for the arts in me at an early age and always being proud of my talents, even though they'd probably never make me rich.

And I think that's all.

All quotations at the beginning of the chapters are by Harry Truman, unless otherwise noted.

A Cautionary Note

When I wrote this book, I realized I'd have some explaining to do regarding my decision to buy a dog in a pet store rather than providing a stay of execution for one of the multitude of abandoned waifs crowding our animal shelters.

The simple fact of the matter is that Truman found *me*. And, as you will see, found me with the aid of my dead husband's spirit. This was not your ordinary dog/owner meeting; it was a bit of a supernatural miracle, the kind you'd better not argue about if you want to stay on the good side of the Unseen.

This is not, however, to imply that I advocate buying rather than adopting pets. I'm an inveterate animal rescuer by nature; I can't count the stray felines, for instance, to whom I've opened my doors throughout the years, to the point where my home was known as "Hotel Cat." I'm a member and supporter of Best Friends, the remarkable international animal sanctuary based in Kanab, Utah, that has transformed several thousand acres of undeveloped land into a veritable Valhalla for thousands of abused and abandoned animals of every species, assuring them happy, healthy, and love-filled new lives. I don't in any way condone the heinous institution of the puppy mill or any other breeding-for-profit endeavors.

I strongly urge anyone thinking of getting a pet to put your heart and your energy into adopting. With so many wonderful animals simply waiting for a place to put all the love they yearn to give, it makes no sense to spend a big wad on that kitty or doggie in the window. Think of the money, and the life, you'll save. It's a win-win situation.

Having said that, I will nonetheless never regret having wandered into our local pet store that dreary, rainy Christmas following my husband's death and falling head over heels for three pounds of dog that would change my life forever. Love is like that—totally unpredictable. But whether Cupid's crafty arrow hits at the pet store or the pound, one truth remains the same: an animal needs love and care for the rest of its life, and bringing it home is not like buying a new outfit at Macy's on sale day and returning it a week later because you just couldn't stand the color. A life is now in your hands; you've made a commitment that, as one of God's creatures, you're obligated to honor.

There are too many selfish sods out there who think nothing of throwing away their children, let alone their pets, but I'm not one of them and neither are you, so I'm sure you know what I'm saying. Abandon a pet, either emotionally or physically, and you abandon the humane side of yourself. Honor your relationship with your pet and you will not only earn "brownie points in heaven" (to borrow an expression from my dear friend Sister Janet Harris), but your life will be immeasurably enriched.

Take it from me—and Truman.

Mary Beth Crain

I met my husband, Adam Shields, in 1992, when I was an editor at *Santa Barbara Magazine*. I was doing an article on two of Santa Barbara's most illustrious residents, the Irish actor-brothers Barry Fitzgerald and Arthur Shields. Barry Fitzgerald, whom everybody remembers for his Oscar-winning performance as the feisty old superior of the young priest Bing Crosby in *Going My Way*, had lived in Santa Barbara for a number of years, and Arthur Shields, a well-known character actor who was often mistaken for his older brother, had also lived in Santa Barbara, from 1961 until his death in 1970.

During my research I discovered that Arthur Shields had a son, Adam, who was living in Santa Paula, about forty-five miles southeast of Santa Barbara. I wrote him a letter asking if he'd be willing to be interviewed, and when I called to follow up a week later, I was greeted with the sweetest voice I'd ever heard, gentle and refined, its unmistakable Dublin accent still very much intact.

"I'd be happy to talk to you," he said. So I went to Adam's house three days later, and when he opened the door, history was made—*our* history, at any rate. He fell in love with me, he said, before I even stepped into the house. "I never got past your eyes," he told me later. It took me much longer—two days, I think—before I realized that I was in love with him.

Adam was a fascinating man. He had been born in Dublin in 1928, and with his father and uncle being so famous in the theater world (and then in American movies), he remembered luminaries such as William Butler Yeats and Paul Robeson coming to the house for tea. When Adam moved to Hollywood at eighteen after the war to live with his father and stepmother, stars and directors were always at the house. Coming home from Hollywood High in the afternoon, he might find Anne Baxter, or Maureen O'Hara, or John Ford in his living room. Once, he recalled with a chuckle, a tall, handsome young man was there, talking to his dad about the next film they were going to do together. Adam happened to mention to this fellow how silly he thought American football was compared to its Irish equivalent. The young man, who had been a football star in college, obligingly took Adam out in the backyard and taught him the basics of the game. It wasn't until Adam saw one of his father's recent pictures, *The Keys of the Kingdom,* that he realized he'd been talking to Gregory Peck.

Adam's later life was just as intriguing. After spending twenty years in the aerospace industry, he retired at forty-two to pursue a career as an artist. He painted beautiful, sensitive scenes of Chumash Indian life. A girl turning into a soaring hawk, a child looking into a lake and seeing his reflection as a strong, grown man, an old woman sitting on a log with a twinkle in her eye, listening to her little grandson describe an adventure—scenes rich in fantasy and mystery, yet rendered so sparingly that I dubbed them visual haiku.

That first day we talked from six in the evening until six the next morning. We even forgot to have dinner! Nothing like that had ever happened to me before—or, it turned out, to him. I thought he was a regular chatterbox until he and everyone else in his family told me that he was generally extremely quiet and reserved, the last person you'd ever in a million years imagine blabbing for twelve hours straight and hardly stopping for breath.

Of course, under the circumstances, this wasn't entirely surprising. Adam was a widower who had lost his wife of thirty-seven years. He'd lived alone the past five years, grieving and reclusive, not looking for another relationship, not daring to think that love could come to him again at the age of sixty-four. As the first woman whom he'd entertained since his wife's death, I became the unwitting corkscrew that unleashed five years of bottled-up emotions.

I ended up sleeping in Adam's spare bedroom that night—or rather, the next morning. He never made a pass at me—he was far too gentlemanly and old-worldly for that. And also quite shy, since his wife was the only woman he'd ever had. I left later that morning and headed for the magazine, wondering if it had all been a dream. But for the next week I couldn't get this slight, charming, handsome man with the twinkling eyes and the soft Irish brogue out of my mind.

Then, one day, he called and we had another talkathon. This apparently was another first. By his own admission, and that of his sister and kids, Adam had inherited his father's almost pathological dislike of telephones and was the master of the one-minute phone conversation.

"I really don't understand what's happening," he said, after an hour had breezed by. "It's as if I've known you for a hundred years."

"I know," I said. And so, a few days later, I went back to Santa Paula for an official date. Adam answered the door, as calm and courtly as you please, and confided to me only later that he'd been glued to the window, waiting for the exhilarating sight of my red Toyota Camry pulling into the driveway.

Again we talked nonstop—this time until 5:30 A.M. Again we missed dinner. And again I slept in the spare bedroom.

I awoke several hours later, thoroughly confused. I knew that we were madly attracted to each other. But Adam had never so much as touched me. What did he want? What did *I* want?

Just as I was about to leave for the magazine I said, "Well Adam, it's been great. Thanks for another wonderful marathon."

And then this cool, collected Irishman held out his arms to me. As I hugged him, I realized that he was shaking.

"I know you're a young kid and I'm an old geezer," he said, trembling. "I have four children who are your age. But if I let you go out that door, you might go out of my life. And I couldn't have that. I'm too much in love with you, you see."

I stroked his hair as if I'd been doing it for twenty years. Everything about him felt so familiar to me—his arms, his eyes, his voice. To this day I can't explain any of it, except to say that I've since ended up believing in past lives.

"I love you too," I said, and then we kissed, and kissed, and kissed . . .

I moved in the next day. We were married a year later, in November, although we always celebrated August 20 as the day we fell in love and the day Adam officially came back to life. I never felt the twenty-three-year age gap between us, and

A Widow, a Chihuahua, and Harry Truman

Adam was genuinely amused when people asked him if I was his daughter.

It's not exaggerating to say that our marriage was made in heaven. We lived in a rarified atmosphere of constant delight. To give you an idea of the kind of man I married, every morning he cut a rose from our garden and had it waiting for me in a vase by the bed when I awoke.

And then Adam died of lung cancer, on August 20, 1996, exactly four years to the day and the hour from when he'd first declared his love to me.

He died at home, in my arms. When they took his wasted body away, my spirit seemed to slip out of me as well. Thus began a period I refer to as my zombiedom, a time when I was like the walking dead, moving through life but not daring to feel. For awhile I even forgot what Adam looked like, because if I let myself remember, the agony was so excruciating that I immediately went numb, the body's way of coping with unbearable pain.

I really don't know what would have happened to me if it hadn't been for Harry Truman and a little dog. Which is where this story really begins.

Chapter 1

Harry Truman and Me

I was sworn in one night and the next morning I had to get right on the job at hand. I was plenty scared, but, of course, I didn't let anybody see it, and I knew I wouldn't be called on to do anything that I wasn't capable of doing.

From as far back as I can remember, I've felt a closeness to Harry Truman. This can undoubtedly be explained, on one level, by the fact that he and my favorite grandfather, Lou Bretstein, looked so much alike that they could have been candidates for that separated-at-birth thing.

This is a bit of an irony considering that Papa Louie was the only rabid Republican in a family crawling with liberal Jewish Democrats. In fact, as the story goes, he got so excited on election eve, 1948, that he forsook his usual temperance to get stinking drunk and slide down the banister yelling, "Hooray for Dewey!" at the top of his lungs.

But the grandfather fixation really takes up only a small amount of space in a heart full of reverence for Harry. His great fortitude, coupled with a level of integrity unheard of in politics and rare enough outside of it, impressed me so much that during the tough times in my life I somehow found myself turning to him for courage and inspiration.

I remember one time a few years back, when things were really bad. My mother was undergoing surgery and I had to travel three thousand miles to be with her, leaving Adam, who was inexplicably under the weather with what turned out to be terminal cancer, on his own. No sooner had I arrived than my brother, who was supposed to come from Michigan to help out with my mother, ended up in a hospital emergency room in Grand Rapids after nearly severing part of his hand. To make matters worse, I'd just had a book deal fall through. Ah, the timing of the universe.

I spent ten hours a day in the hospital with my mom, after which I'd go back to her house and collapse. "Do something nice for yourself," my aunt advised me one evening over the phone from Florida. "Go out to dinner at a nice restaurant. Treat yourself."

Hmm. I thought about what would make me feel really good. Then I made myself a hot dog and sat down with *Plain Speaking*, Merle Miller's book of conversations with Harry Truman, which just happened to be staring at me from one of my mother's overloaded bookshelves.

I was soon reminded that Harry Truman was no stranger to adversity. Nothing ever seemed to come easily to him. He toughed it out when his father died, putting his own dreams on hold to take over the family farm. He weathered the First World War as Captain Truman, heroic leader of men in battle. He endured the terror of financial ruin when a failed business enterprise plunged him into debt with a wife and child to support. And his political life was one long, arduous climb up an endless mountain of scorn and contempt—attitudes that metamorphosed into reverence only years after he left the White House and people finally recognized the remarkable qualities that had made him one of our greatest presidents.

Yet all Harry had to say, when asked about the tough times, was, "What I did was what I had to do. . . . And I always went ahead and did it as best I could without taking time out to worry about how it would have been if it had worked out another way. Or to complain about what happened. You'll notice, if you read your history, that the work of the world gets done by people who aren't bellyachers."

Oh, brother. I could sense Harry's finger pointing right at me. I'd been feeling pretty sorry for myself this past week, I had to admit. Why? Because I wanted things to be different. I wanted my mother and brother and husband to be okay. I wanted that book deal to go through. I wanted life to be permanent-press. But life, like people, gets wrinkles. That's what it's all about. And I realized in that moment that Harry Truman's great strength came from the fact that he never *expected* life to be easy. So he was never disappointed or thrown for a loop when the sea got rough. You could say that he came into this world with his philosophical life preserver on, and it kept him afloat for eighty-eight years.

"You can't always do what you'd like to do," Harry reminded me, from another page. "And the sooner you learn that, the better off everybody is."

Those words instantly made me feel better, calmer, as though I'd taken a couple of Extra-Strength Excedrin. Extra-Strength Truman, that's what it was. And so, for the rest of the week, I consumed hot dogs and the wisdom of Harry Truman every night, and I must say I couldn't have done anything nicer for myself.

When Adam died, though, even Harry couldn't make me feel better. Maybe it was because the one tough thing he'd never had to face was losing Bess. Considering how much he loved her, he might not have been able to make it without her, although my instinct tells me that he would eventually have gotten up and dusted himself off and gone on just as he always had, a little emptier inside, perhaps, but still in the ring till God himself took him out.

But I needed something stronger than Extra-Strength Truman to get me through this one. Something that would either numb me forever or bring me back to life. Something that would make me remember what joy felt like. Something miraculous, something magical, something I couldn't believe existed. Something like . . . a chihuahua?

Chapter 2

The Meeting

I certainly don't think a man has to be big and tall,
has to have a commanding appearance and a good
height, in order to be a good president.

One cold December day, just before my first Christmas
following Adam's death, I decided to go to the best place for
jump-starting one's soul: the pet store.

Whenever I was down in the dumps, Adam would remark,
with that gentle twinkle in his Irish eyes, "Somebody needs a
kitten fix," or, "I say, love, why don't we go down to the pet
shop and pick up a six-pack of kittens?" And off we would go
to Pet Headquarters, where I would lose myself in a sea of tiny
furry faces and where, if I was lucky, they'd let me hold a kitten, even though they knew I had no intention of buying it. I
already had three big, spoiled cats, and the last kitten I'd taken
home from Pet Headquarters had had to be returned because
they had almost eaten it alive.

On this particular afternoon I entered Pet Headquarters
hoping to see Woodrow, an abandoned kitten who had been

all alone for the last week. I felt a kinship with Woodrow, whom I had named after Woodrow Wilson, another of my favorite chiefs of state, because in these sordid and illiterate times it's a happy thought that our country was actually once run by the president of Princeton.

Woodrow, it turned out, had been adopted the previous day, which made me happy because he'd have a home for Christmas, but sad because I'd really needed a kitten fix at that particular moment. That's when I noticed that the puppy play-pen was open and a teensy little chihuahua was staring in my direction, head cocked, one ear drooping, the other standing at attention.

I'd never owned a dog. But lately—say, in the last couple of years—I'd been thinking about one. I had misty, romantic images of a faithful companion that did everything you wanted it to, lived to be dressed up in T-shirts and hats, and was generally the antithesis of my cats.

This strange shift in allegiance hadn't been pleasing to my husband, who'd had little use for dogs, classifying them into two categories: woofers and tweeters. When I'd mentioned that I thought a chihuahua might be fun, he'd been horrified. A nasty, yippy little tweeter? It was unthinkable. And besides, it would compromise the cats' dignity. End of discussion.

But shortly after Adam passed away, our male live-in aide, a young Salvadoran by the name of David, told me that toward the end my husband had confided to him, "After I die, I know that Mary Beth's going to get a chihuahua."

"Did he really say that?" I asked. I began to cry, feeling terrible. What did he think, that I couldn't wait for him to expire so I could get a chihuahua?

"No, no," David said, laughing. "He just know you want a

chihuahua." But he was as mystified over my obsession as Adam had been. "Why you want a chihuahua?" he said. "Is not a dog; is a rat!"

I wandered over to the puppy playpen to get a closer look. This was the tiniest dog I had ever seen. He tipped the bird-seed scale at three pounds. His tail was the size of my index finger. You'd need a magnifying glass to see his teeth and toes. I couldn't believe he was for real.

The store clerk, sensing a bona fide sucker, smiled at me and uttered the fatal words, "Want to hold him?"

Knowing better, *much* better, I nodded. She scooped up the black-and-cream ball of tweeter and handed him to me. He felt weightless, and I handled him as gingerly as if he'd been made of spun glass. I put him against my cheek and he rested there, just as quiet and calm as you please. None of those nervous tremors and bug-eyed looks of terror one traditionally associates with chihuahuas, a neurotic breed that my pet-sitter, Pat, ominously referred to as "ankle-biters" when I called her that evening for advice on whether or not to buy the dog.

"What the hail do you want a chee-wa-wa for?" she inquired in her blunt Oklahoma drawl. "They hate feet. That's because they're all the time gettin' stepped on. So they go for ankles. Plus they're bred to be with you, and I mean *with* you, twenty-four hours a day. If you're out of their sight for one minute they start wailin' like they're fixin' to die. You'll be *wearin'* that dog."

I kissed the puppy on his silky little head, and he looked up at me with two big, soft fawn eyes. When a tiny tongue began to lick me shyly, it was basically all over. The store clerk grinned, and I felt like the bull's-eye on a dartboard.

"How much is he?" I asked.

"Six hundred."

"*Dollars?*"

She nodded, looking me over as if I were the village idiot. "He's a *purebred*, you know."

Wow! That came to two hundred dollars a pound. We're talking an expensive cut here.

"I'll think about it," I said, handing the puppy back to her. He began to whimper as she set him down, and I almost whipped out my credit card on the spot. Summoning Herculean strength, I restrained myself. You can't get a dog, I told myself sternly. You've just finished months of being a twenty-four-hour-a-day caretaker. You're trying to sell the house. You travel too much. You need a break from responsibility. And besides, you have three cats who'd swallow this little fellow like an aspirin. So get the hell out of here before you do something really stupid.

My lecture worked. Temporarily, anyway. I walked out of the store puppyless and all the stronger for it. For two weeks I heroically kept away from Pet Headquarters, as an alcoholic on the wagon might recoil from the tempting sight of the neighborhood bar. In the meantime I asked everyone who called for their opinion. All my friends who were dog owners cheered me on to get the puppy. "The perfect cure for grief," they assured me. All my friends who *weren't* dog owners told me I was out of my mind. "What do you need *that* for now?"

Finally my therapist decided the issue. "You need something to change your environment," she said, when I told her how depressed I was being in the house without Adam.

"What do you think about a puppy?" I asked.

"I think it's a *great* idea," she replied. "I think it's just what you need right now. Something to love, something to distract you, something to make you laugh again."

Laughter? What was that? I had forgotten. Those first holidays after Adam's death were the most difficult I've ever experienced. The days were chilly and gray, the nights black holes of loneliness. I lapsed back into the first stage of grief—denial—and found myself refusing to believe that my husband, my soul, my very life, was dead. He *couldn't* have left me forever, not with Christmas coming. He'd never do that to me.

I felt lost, rootless. Several days a week I worked at a newspaper in L.A., and often I'd stay late into the night, long after my work was done, playing solitaire on the computer, dreading the long drive home to the now dark and empty house. I would cry most of the way home, tears fogging my vision. Out of sheer desperation I began fantasizing that Adam would be there when I arrived, to welcome me home as he always had, with a cup of coffee, a sandwich, and a bear hug. Magical thinking, they call it. On such nights I was devastated when I opened the door, only to be greeted by the strange, shifting shadows the moonlight cast through the slats in the blinds and a silence as final as death itself.

I began having eerie, hallucinatory experiences. More than once, when I walked into the house, I thought I saw the top of Adam's head peeping up from his favorite big recliner. I had dreams where I found him sitting in his chair and threw myself into his arms—dreams so vivid that when I awoke I could smell the sweet scent of his hair and feel the softness of his plaid flannel shirt.

Who then could blame me for wanting to sleep more and more? I was reminded of a story that a troubled friend of mine who had committed suicide at the age of twenty-six had told me about a stay she'd once had in the UCLA psychiatric ward. In the ward was a young woman who, in a drug-induced state of temporary insanity, had put out her own eyes. She slept all the time, day and night; it was all they could do to keep her awake long enough to feed her. Everyone thought she was a vegetable, until one day she revealed to my friend that she slept because the only place she could see again was in her dreams.

Was *I* going mad? Sometimes I thought so. The pain of my loss was so intense, so immense, that it seemed to devour me. I was tired much of the time, like a swimmer caught in a riptide, struggling to keep from going under. I had to keep going; there was no one to support me, no savings to cushion me. But the effort it took simply to go to work, do the shopping, pay the bills grew and grew, until I began to fear that the riptide would claim me and I would indeed drown in the great, vast sea of grief, the biggest ocean in the world, with no beginning and no end.

I guess this was one Christmas I could be excused for forgetting people's gifts, not sending out cards, and generally withdrawing from the world. But when, on the night before Christmas Eve, I realized that I hadn't yet gotten my brother *The Tibetan Book of Living and Dying*, which he'd really been wanting, I felt serious pangs of guilt. Why not just get it over with?

The rain was pouring down in sheets. A person had to be crackers to drive on the dark, waterlogged streets on one of the busiest shopping evenings of the year. I considered putting my errand off, but something wouldn't let me. That something poked and prodded at my conscience until I succumbed, grabbed an umbrella, and headed out. My plan was to dash into Barnes & Noble and dash out, shielding my eyes from the

A Widow, a Chihuahua, and Harry Truman

festive holiday atmosphere as a vampire tries to ward off the deadly sunrise.

I found the book within three minutes and was about to leave when, again, that strange something gripped me. This time it wouldn't let me go. Instead, it began pushing me toward the section on grief. While this seemed quite stupid, as I'd been a frequenter of that area and couldn't imagine that anything new would have come in since my last visit, I turned down the aisle anyway, almost stepping on a young woman sitting cross-legged on the floor.

She was a pretty little thing, delicate, with fine features and long dark hair, and when she looked up, her clear blue eyes seemed to be staring past me, into another world.

"Have you lost someone recently?" she asked, in a soft voice.

"Yes. My husband."

"Oh. I'm sorry."

"And you?"

"My father." She continued to leaf through a book she'd been reading, and suddenly she said, "I'm psychic, you know."

Uh-huh, I thought. You and everybody else in L.A.

"People call me an angel."

Even though I've co-authored three angel books and have had some interesting angel experiences of my own, I was wary. After you join the angel book brigade, you suddenly become a dumping ground for the stories of everybody who thinks he or she is an angel, or has met an angel, or is talking on a regular basis to the heavenly host. The Archangel Michael, for instance, is apparently particularly chatty: I can't tell you how many letters my co-author Terry Lynn Taylor and I have received from excited readers sure that they, and they alone, have been picked as his personal channel. So when it comes to angels, I've learned to be discriminating.

"I like to help people," she went on. "I've helped a lot of people. I tell them all about their lives and I never charge them anything. God told me it's a gift that was given to me, so I have to give it to others."

My caution was beginning to evaporate. There was something so sweet, so pure, about her.

"I think I'm getting a message from your husband," she said. "Did he look like this?" And she began describing Adam with stunning accuracy.

"I . . . yes. Yes, that's him." I was seized by an attack of goosebumps as she calmly continued.

"He's very happy," she said. "He's surrounded by flowers. He loves you and doesn't want you to be sad. Wait, now he's showing me your house. It's kind of pink—"

A year earlier I'd had our house painted a sandy pink.

"—with a yellow sign in front of it."

I had just put the house on the market, a wrenching decision for me, and the yellow "For Sale" sign had gone up the week before. When I had first seen it, I'd collapsed in tears, sobbing to Adam to forgive me for having to move on from the house he had lived in and loved for twenty-six years.

"Yes," I said. "I just put the house up for sale."

"Your husband wants you to know it's okay to sell the house," she said. "He understands."

I knelt down beside this small being, whom I judged to be no more than seventeen.

A Widow, a Chihuahua, and Harry Truman

"What's your name?" I asked.

"Andrea."

"How old are you, Andrea?"

"Twenty-five." She smiled, and her face was suffused with radiance. "Your husband loves you so much! It must have been beautiful, what you had."

"It was," I replied, trying to keep back the tears.

"Well, he's still around. He's with you a lot! Do you have a white minivan?"

After Adam had been diagnosed, I'd bought a white Ford Windstar, a gorgeous vehicle that combined the virtues of spaceship luxury with plenty of room for the wheelchair, walker, and oxygen tank that would soon become cumbersome additions to our lives. Adam was crazy about the Windstar; every time he got into it, he'd invariably exclaim, "God! I love this car!"

"Well, whenever you're driving, your husband is sitting right there beside you," Andrea informed me. "And he *loves* that car! He's telling me that."

She was really on a roll now. She told me that I'd been missing my medication and that Adam wanted me to be sure to take it. I was on meds for high blood pressure, and during the last month, brain-fogged with grief, I'd been forgetting to take my pills—an unconscious sign, no doubt, of not really wanting to be around anyway.

"Your husband's very concerned," Andrea admonished me. "He says you have to stay healthy because you've still got a lot to do."

She rose. "I have to meet my friend over there," she said, pointing to the Starbucks on the premises. "Come on. I want to introduce you to her."

We walked over to the café, where I was introduced to a nice-looking woman in her early thirties.

"This is Daisy. I met her at Target last year," Andrea said. "She was standing over by the jewelry, and all of a sudden her father started talking to me and telling me to go over to her. He told me his name was Tom and he wanted to let her know he was okay. Well, it was pretty weird, but I went over to this total stranger and said, 'Excuse me, is your father named Tom?' And she just stared at me, and then she started to cry, because, see, he'd just died."

"Man, was I freaked!" said Daisy, laughing. "Out of the blue, here she comes. And she describes my dad and everything."

"I gave her a whole bunch of messages from him, and we've been real good friends ever since. Tom still comes by a lot."

"Yeah," said Daisy. "You can always tell when he's in the room because the lights go off and on. He's the practical-joker type."

I figured this was all worth, at the very least, a couple of cappuccinos. I bought one for Andrea and on she went, caffeine-propelled into home run after home run in the psychic accuracy ballpark. She described Adam's favorite bathrobe—the big fuzzy one I'd bought him—and said that he wanted me to wear it because I'd feel closer to him. She described the entire interior of our house, from the new carpets and floors to the attached garage and laundry room.

"He's showing me your washer and dryer," she said. "They're sort of green."

Yes, avocado to be exact, ancient relics from 1968.

Then Andrea looked at me intently.

"Do you have a little dog?" she asked.

A Widow, a Chihuahua, and Harry Truman

I froze. "Not yet," I said.

"But you're thinking about getting one, right?"

I nodded.

"Your husband likes that little dog! He wants you to get it."

"Are you sure?" It seemed bizarre. "He always hated little dogs."

"Oh, but he likes this one!" She giggled, a tinkly, little-girl giggle. "He says he helped you to find him. They get real busy over there after they arrive, you know. They have all sorts of assignments, to help people they loved on earth and make up with people they didn't. Your husband's a quick learner. He'll do real well. He managed to get you and me together tonight— that was pretty awesome."

"How did he do that?"

"Well, it's complicated. I mean, first he had to send a psychic suggestion to you, to drive over here. Then he had to send one to me. I wasn't planning on coming here tonight; Daisy here will tell you."

"That's right," Daisy agreed, nodding. "We were just cruisin' around when all of a sudden this one says, 'Pull in to Barnes & Noble.' And I go, 'Why?' and she says, 'I don't know. I just think I've gotta go in there.' Man, I tell you, with Andrea you never know where you're going to end up."

"And then he had to get us together," Andrea continued, "once we were in the store. That takes coordination! I bet he's pretty proud of himself right now."

I felt like I was going to levitate right there in the middle of Barnes & Noble. Adam was *with* me! I mean, how could you argue with a phenomenon like Andrea? I wanted to hug her. Instead, I said, "Hey, Andrea, I'm sort of into astrology. When's your birthday?"

"January 26," she replied.

Oh, no. It couldn't be.

"That's *my* birthday," I said.

"It is?" She was delighted. "What year were you born?"

"1951. And you?"

"1971." She gazed at me happily. "You could be my mother. I never really had a mother."

"I guess I could. Only I feel more like *you* could be *mine*. You're so incredibly wise."

"Oh, that's just God, talking through me," she said, shrugging. "I screw up a lot, don't worry."

I drove back home in a daze, almost backing the Windstar into a wall as I pulled out of the parking lot. I probably was in no condition to drive, especially in the rain at midnight, but I figured that if Adam was in the car with me, he sure as hell wouldn't let me crash. After all, I still had a lot left to do before I checked out of Hotel Earth.

That Christmas Eve a transformation took place deep inside of me. I had met an angel, a genuine messenger from my husband. I felt protected, guided. I realized that while there are plenty of mysteries, there are no accidents, and no mistakes. My life was unfolding according to a plan, and part of that plan included getting a chihuahua puppy.

Why, I had no idea. But apparently Adam did.

Chapter 3

The Cats

Every president inherits the problems
of the last administration.

As I debated the pros and cons of dog ownership, my cats clearly realized that something was up, because suddenly, without warning, they went into their best dog acts. They whined. They licked my hand. They trailed me from room to room with pathetic eyes. I swear to God this is true. Just because I'd decided that while cats are great in their own way, they don't come when you call them or slobber all over you or jump in the car with you or sleep plastered against you. Petie, my big black-and-white male cat, came bounding from across the street at the sound of my voice; Rhonda, my gray-and-orange tabby, crawled into my bed in the middle of the night, licked me all over, and fell asleep on my stomach; and Angel, their mother, jumped into the car and plopped down on the front seat with such doglike ease that I half-expected her to put her paws on the window and start panting.

Mother of God. They'd pushed the guilt button, and it worked. My only defense was that I was a new widow and therefore not responsible for my actions as I stuffed them with their favorite treats, feeling like Benedict Arnold every time I thought of the little chihuahua. One night, as Petie lay next to me in bed with his paw in my hand, I finally vowed to give up the whole dog idea—which was, of course, their ultimate telepathic goal.

But every time I closed my eyes I saw that innocent, adorable little face. It wouldn't be so bad to go back and take just one more *peek* at the puppy, would it? Like, yeah, I can stop at one drink; watch me. So, a few days later, toward closing time on New Year's Eve, I went back to Pet Headquarters, just to see if he'd been taken. I was completely philosophical. If he had, it was God's will. And if he hadn't . . .

He hadn't. In fact, when he saw me approaching his playpen he threw himself against the glass and began jumping up and down like one of those windup toys. Was it just my unreliable new widow's imagination, or did this little squirt actually *recognize* me?

"We knew you'd be back," said the store owner, Laurie, beaming as she unlocked the playpen door. The puppy tumbled into my arms and began to lick me frantically.

"I guess you're going home with me," I said, strangely relieved. Instead of feeling that I was taking on a burden, I felt that one had been lifted from me.

"We knew you and he were perfect for each other!" Laurie trilled. "Have you decided what you're going to name him?"

"Yeah. Truman."

"Truman? After Truman Capote?"

God forbid! "No. After *Harry* Truman."

A Widow, a Chihuahua, and Harry Truman

"Well, he's a Truman, all right."

I held Truman up, all three whopping pounds of him.

"Truman," I said, "you are a fine young man."

I suddenly noticed that a Mexican family—two children, mother, father, and grandmother—had been staring at me.

"Did you buy the chihuahua?" the little boy asked me. I nodded.

"How much?" the mother wanted to know.

"Six hundred dollars."

The mother relayed this information in Spanish to the grandmother, who clapped a hand to her mouth with a long "Ayeeee" and stared at me as if I were either J. Paul Getty or certifiably loco. She was still shaking her head in wonder as they left the store, chattering to each other in heated Spanish that sounded like a scolding. Six hundred dollars! Six hundred dollars for a canine burrito you couldn't pay somebody to take off your hands on the other side of the border. I felt like a total fool.

It was a feeling I was going to have to learn to get used to. The reality of the situation was beginning to sink in. What had I done? How the hell was I going to take care of a dog? I suddenly felt the cold terror of a new mother bringing her baby home from the hospital. The words of Prissy in *Gone with the Wind* floated back to me, with a slight revision: "I don' know nothin' 'bout raisin' chihuahuas, Miz Scarlett!"

"Don't worry," Laurie assured me. "He'll be real easy to take care of."

Uh-huh.

On the advice of Cissy, the store assistant, I bought a kennel; an armload of the most expensive canned puppy food in the store; a guidebook to Your New Chihuahua; a bag of dry dog food that was three times the size of Truman; a pack of Puppy Wee-Wee Pads, a guaranteed aid to painless housebreaking; a bag of smoked, dried pig ears that were revolting to behold; a red turtleneck sweater; and numerous puppy toys, including a tinkly bone, a chewy rope, and a squeaky Santa. I drew the line at a little bandanna with red and green Christmas trees all over it.

"I just thought you'd want to dress him up for the holidays," Cissy explained.

Excuse me—I forgot the Puppy Car Seat. Yes, a tiny little canvas seat that hooks onto the passenger seat and holds puppy in with a belt and buckle. Cissy demonstrated the wonders of this indispensable invention by installing it in a shopping cart, strapping Truman in, and wheeling him all over the store. Truman stood up on his little hind legs and viewed the world as he went sailing down the aisles, to the great delight of the customers.

"See?" said Cissy. "He can stand up in his seat and look out the window and everything."

Why not? I took the car seat. The total bill came to nearly eight hundred dollars. The foolish feeling intensified.

Amid fond and tender farewells, Truman left the pet store and embarked upon his new life. It was an auspicious way to ring in the New Year. Everybody was waving and calling out, "Goodbye, Truman; good luck!" like the crowds standing at the dock as an ocean liner sets out to sea. In this case, I was praying that it wasn't the *Titanic*. Since everything I knew about puppies could fit nicely into a grasshopper's hip pocket, and there were three cats at home who might very well take one look at Truman and think, "Dinner!" the potential for disaster was not entirely imaginary.

A Widow, a Chihuahua, and Harry Truman

Actually, disaster reared its ugly head not two minutes after Laurie's son, Steve, had strapped Truman into his little car seat and left me alone for the first time with what the puppy instruction books quaintly refer to as the New Arrival. It was chilly, dark, and rainy, and poor Truman didn't have his sweater on. So, in addition to being completely disoriented and terrified, he was shivering with cold. "Hang on, sweetie," I said, reaching over to turn on the heat. "You'll be warm in no time. And we'll be home just as fast."

But my soothing words didn't have the desired effect. As soon as the car started moving, Truman erupted in a concert of heartrending wails, rattling me so that I narrowly missed a stop sign and had to slam on the brakes. This sudden jolt sent Truman over the edge. He struggled frantically to get out of his puppy seat and managed to get his front paw through the chest strap, whereupon he began to choke. His wails escalated into strangled yelps that sent me veering into the nearest gas station, yelling, "Hang on, Truman! Hang on!"

Christ! Could a brand-new puppy die on a six-minute drive home? I jumped out of the car and went to his rescue. But as I tried to free Truman he only struggled harder, causing me to fumble ineptly with his safety strap. Finally I extricated him from the puppy seat of death and returned to the driver's seat, where I held him in one hand and steered with the other. This was probably totally insane, but compared to what we'd just been through, it seemed like a piece of cake. Truman whimpered the rest of the way home, however, making me feel like Cruella De Vil. Thank God there weren't 101 of him!

I screeched into the driveway, gripped the New Arrival tightly, stepped out of the car, and stopped dead in my tracks. Damn it. The cats. I'd originally planned to smuggle Truman in during the day, when the monsters were snoozing in the backyard, soaking up their regular afternoon rays. But it was six-thirty now, past their dinnertime, which meant that they'd all be lined up like a firing squad at the door. There was only one thing to be done: I hid Truman in my jacket, rushed into the house, and made a dash for the spare bedroom, slamming the door in three confused feline faces. Then I promptly collapsed on the futon couch.

Truman peeped out mournfully from my armpit. I set him down on the couch and told him to be a good boy while I went back to the car to get his things. Again my instructions went unheeded. As I slipped out of the bedroom to face three pairs of suspicious yellow-and-green eyes, Truman began to wail.

Petie looked at me with what could only be described as shock and disapproval. Rhonda hunkered down and began that menacing feline rumble that precedes war. And Angel bolted, zooming down the hall, into the kitchen, up on the counter, and through the open window, scattering dishes right and left in her frenzied flight.

I carted the kennel in and set up the nursery. I put Truman's food and water down and tried coaxing him with the squeaky Santa, but he was too scared to do anything but whimper. So I held him and talked to him and he huddled in my hands, tail hidden between his legs—a response that, according to the chihuahua book, meant that he wasn't a happy camper. That book would rapidly become my bible. In the ensuing weeks I consulted it at least thirty times a day. Since it is as the jacket proclaimed, the "#1 Bestselling Chihuahua Book," I guess you could call it the chihuahua's Dr. Spock.

After about half an hour Truman began venturing about.

A Widow, a Chihuahua, and Harry Truman

Soon he was exploring the room with gusto, sniffing in every corner. His tail was beginning to stick up like a little question mark—the sign, said the book, of a happy chihuahua. There were, however, two decidedly unhappy cats still camped out at the door to the Forbidden City. When I went out to check on them, *their* tails were flicking back and forth in true pissed-off cat fashion.

"Listen, you guys," I said earnestly, beginning the lecture I'd planned to deliver before the New Arrival ever arrived. "You've got a new baby brother."

Silence. Flick, flick, flick went the tails.

"He's just a puppy and he won't hurt you. All he wants to do is play. Now you know I'll always love you best, don't you?"

Flick, flick, flick.

"But Mommy needed a puppy. Don't ask me to explain. Just don't eat him, okay?"

I bent down to stroke them. Petie turned away from me wrathfully. Rhonda began to growl. Truman chimed in helpfully from behind the door. I called my pet-sitter.

"Pat," I said. "I bought the chihuahua."

"Ma!" she yelled to her mother, who was visiting and who had once owned an ankle-biter. "She went and did it! She bought the damn chee-wa-wa!"

"Uh, Pat, listen. Truman's in the spare bedroom. Angel's bolted, and Petie and Rhonda are *not* amused. I haven't introduced them yet, but they know something fishy is behind that door. So what do you suggest?"

"Introduce 'em gradually," she said, with great authority. "Make sure he's in his crate, and then let them come in and sniff at him. Talk real sweet to the cats. Tell 'em you love 'em and that he's just a baby and they need to protect him. After a few days they'll get the idea. Oh, my Lord. I can't believe you went ahead and did it."

"Yeah. And Truman cries every time I leave the room."

"What did I tell you? I *told* you he'd want to be with you all the time, didn't I? You'll just have to outlast it. For the love of God I can't figure out how anybody lives through puppy-hood. You're in for it, honey."

On this encouraging note I returned to the nursery. Truman was sniffing and turning around in circles. The action jogged my memory; I'd read, when leafing through the book, that dogs did that when they were getting ready to you-know-what. Quickly I opened the package of wee-wee pads and threw one on the floor. The package said that they contained a special scent that would "encourage" the puppy to eliminate on them. Sure enough, Truman went over and sniffed the pad with interest. Then he promptly peed on the rug.

Oh, well. I did what the book said to do and put Truman on the pad, hoping to make the connection between "wee-wee" and "wee-wee pad" in his walnut-sized brain. "Good dog," I said. "Good boy. Wee-wee on the pad."

Truman looked up at me happily, jumped off the pad, and went behind the TV. The next thing I knew, an unsavory smell was wafting over in my direction.

"Oh, shit," I groaned, not inappropriately. I got on my hands and knees and peered behind the TV. There were two tiny puppy turds on the floor. Truman watched me with great interest—possibly even pride—as I cleaned them up. Later I would read in a number of puppy training books, "Never let the dog see you clean his mess. He'll think you're his maid." Advantage Truman.

A Widow, a Chihuahua, and Harry Truman

I was so absorbed in getting Truman situated that I hardly noticed that the year was coming to an end. The sound of fireworks reminded me that this was the first New Year's Eve since Adam's death and that I was going to go to bed alone and wake up alone (unless I counted a three-pound chihuahua as a substitute for the husband I didn't know how I was going to live without). I lay there with Truman on the futon couch in the room where Adam had died and gazed out the window. The sky was dizzy with stars; the leaves of the trees were awash in moonlight. I began to cry. Then I heard a tiny, mournful whimper and found myself under the scrutiny of two anxious puppy eyes.

"Oh, my God," I thought. "I'm freaking this dog out."

But suddenly I felt a sloppy little tongue on my cheek, licking away the tears. This made me cry all the harder, which in turn made him whimper all the louder, until we sounded like a couple of keeners at a wake. I fell asleep like that, Truman curled up under my chin, and when I woke up it was 1997 and I actually had a reason to go on living. The reason had just poked its head out of the covers and was stretching its Popsicle-stick legs and yawning, revealing a mouthful of pin-sized teeth that were headed in the direction of my nose. Ouch! It was breakfast time.

Chapter 4

Angel

I said, "It has been said about you that you have stood by a man to the last drop of mercy." Mr. Truman replied, "I would rather have that said about me than to be a great man."

—*William Hillman*, Harry S. Truman

Our cat Angel was Adam's best friend. When he was ill, she was truly an Angel of Mercy, standing by him "to the last drop of mercy," worthy of the Harry Truman Award for Steadfast Loyalty.

She had always been an odd creature. The very fact of her existence was a miracle; when I'd come across her, five years earlier, in a pet store where I'd gone to get some cat food, she was four weeks old and smaller than my hand, the only kitten left of an orphaned litter that had been dumped at the store after the mother had died of poisoning. But as tiny as she was, Angel had a remarkable pair of lungs. Standing on her hind feet, microscopic front paws gripping the cage, she emitted a series of strident screeches that would have startled a drill sergeant, staring straight at me the whole time. The unmistakable message was, "Where the hell have you been? Get me out of here! Now!"

Anyone's heart would have melted at the sight of this itsy-bitsy scrapper, all by herself in the big lonely cage, already eating dry food when she still should have been nursing, fighting loudly and determinedly for her life. So of course I, being the patron saint of strays, went in for a bag of cat food and walked out with another cat.

But when I took Angel to the vet, he somberly pronounced her not long for this world. "Kittens that little, taken from their mother, usually don't survive," he warned, shaking his head sadly as he examined her ears and she let loose with an ear-splitting yowl that was easily ten times her size.

I wasn't so sure. She'd made it this far on sheer force of will, and she certainly seemed healthy enough. Not willing to make funeral arrangements just yet, I took her back home, fed her kitten formula, and endured the usual pain-in-the-ass rite of passage as my older cat, Snicky, hissed and spat at the tiny pretender to the throne. I kept them apart for a week or so, until, one unforgettable day, Angel jumped on top of Snicky and rode her like a horse, paws wrapped around her neck. I was sure Snicky would kill her right then and there, but to my astonishment she merely growled grumpily and accepted the role of Angel's steed, plodding around the house as Angel hung on for dear life and chirped with delight.

Not quite a year later, Angel, who had grown into a small, beautiful cat, gave birth to a big, brawny litter of five. I kept Petie and Rhonda and settled into life with a family of four felines. Snicky died at thirteen, not long after I met Adam, and Angel and the babies took over the house and our hearts. To our surprise, Angel, who had always been wild at heart and could never be accused of lowering herself to the level of laptop cat, adopted Adam as her person. Although she hated being picked up and almost never curled up with me, she would jump into Adam's lap and put her paws around his stomach, purring in bliss as he beamed from ear to ear and vainly tried to feign manly indifference.

Angel was definitely slightly crazy. She preferred flying to walking and would leap ten feet upward to catch a bird in midair, or bound onto the mantel or refrigerator in the blink of an eye. Because of Angel's unusually long hind legs and lean body, Adam was convinced she was part ocelot. One of her favorite activities, when she was outside and wanted in, was to attach herself to a screen. You'd be walking by a window and out of the corner of your eye you'd see this cat, hanging onto the screen by all four paws in cruciform position, frantically trying to get your attention. This prompted Adam to wryly dub her "our star of stage and screen."

As Adam's cancer progressed, Angel refused to leave his side. Sometimes, when the chemo gave him chills, she would curl up next to him in bed, his own personal fur-covered hot-water bottle. Or she would simply sit in his lap, guarding him, so protective that if his disease had been a visible enemy, she would have torn it to shreds.

When Adam grew closer to death, all the cats wanted to be near him. But our two live-in aides—David, whom I mentioned earlier, and his co-worker, Rosa (angels in their own right)—regarded them with deep suspicion; in their Salvadoran culture, cats were considered dangerous, even evil. So, in a noble effort

A Widow, a Chihuahua, and Harry Truman

to protect Adam, David and Rosa mounted an offense that would have been admirable, I suppose, had they understood just who they were dealing with. No matter how assiduously they shooed the enemy out, or how often they made sure to close the bedroom door, the cats would figure out a way in.

I'll never forget the morning I walked into Adam's room to find that he had wet the bed. Who was curled up next to him but big old Petie, who had stolen in during the night and absolutely refused to budge, even though he was lying on soaking-wet sheets.

Poor Angel was the most distraught. A nervous animal, she was as suspicious of David and Rosa as they were of her and would disappear as soon as she saw them. But she was also desperate to be with Adam. Once, when Angel tried to sneak into Adam's room, Rosa saw her and came after her as though she were the devil incarnate.

"Out, cat!" Rosa hissed, and Angel fled.

"She won't hurt him, Rosa," I said, trying to reason with her. "She *loves* him."

"Is no good for Mr. Shields," Rosa insisted. "Cat leaves hair, dirt—not clean."

What the hell it mattered at this late stage I couldn't fathom. But there was no arguing with Rosa, who, bless her heart, was determined to do her duty right down to the last letter of the law.

Imagine my amazement, then, when I went into Adam's room later that night and discovered Angel all snuggled up next to him in the bed, beaming with triumph. How the hell had she gotten in, I wondered? Then I noticed the window. Because it was summer and hot, it was open; and the screen was off its hinges, flapping in the breeze. With dogged (pardon the expression) determination, Angel had obviously attached herself to the screen and torn it off.

"Our star of stage and screen," I laughed, stroking her, while Adam smiled, too weak to talk.

From that moment until Adam died a couple of days later, the cats sat vigil around him, Angel and Petie in the cramped hospital bed, Rhonda on the floor. No dog could have been more devoted, or more devastated when the end finally came. The night Adam died, after the men from the morgue had taken his body away, I found Petie sitting in the empty hospital bed. Crawling in next to him, I explained that Adam had died. Petie stared at me and began to cry—high-pitched, mournful wails, as if his little heart were cracking in two. I held him and cried too.

Each of the cats reacted differently to Adam's death. Rhonda came into the room, looked around nervously, and ran out. And Angel never came in at all; but remained outside, withdrawn in mourning too private to be shared. From that point on, in fact, she rarely surfaced except to eat a few mouthfuls now and again, and she grew thin and depressed. Like a small child who reacts to the death of a parent by retreating into angry, bewildered solitude, Angel was unreachable. I couldn't talk to her the way I could to Petie; she regarded me with sullen distrust no matter how I approached her. Perhaps she blamed me for Adam's death—who knows? Or at least for not managing to keep him alive. While my heart ached for her, there seemed to be nothing I could do, except to be there for her no matter how large the gap between us grew—until it felt, some days, as if I were at one side of the Grand Canyon and she at the other.

Sadness now hung over the house like a shroud. Petie moped around, following me into every room as if afraid that I, too, would disappear forever. Rhonda was her usual neurotic self, only more so, alternating between begging hungrily for petting and running away from me with a terrified look, as though I were a stranger. I cried a lot, slept a lot, and wasn't, I'm afraid, a very good companion to them. It was only when I got Truman, five months later, that life began poking out from me again, like a new shoot of grass tentatively greeting the world with a mixture of uncertainty and hope.

What was the secret of that new life? In a word: laughter.

It's scary how quiet a house becomes after someone dies. Ours was all the more quiet for the contrast: if there was one thing that characterized Adam's and my relationship, it was laughter. My husband had a dryly witty way of looking at the world that was very Irish; he probably would have had Oscar Wilde in stitches. He was a master observer of the ludicrous; once, for instance, when we were in bed and one of the cats decided to walk the entire length of me, starting at my feet, going up my legs and stomach, and finally settling down under my chin, Adam offhandedly remarked, "Do you ever feel like the runway at a cat fashion show?"

When we couldn't sleep, we'd lie in bed making up limericks. Adam would toss me the first line, which he tried to make as fiendishly challenging as possible. Once he thought he had me with "A young man who went to Yosemite . . ." But I won the day with

A young man who went to Yosemite
Returned with a frozen extremity.
He said, "Ain't it grand, that it's only my hand,
For my ____ would have been a calamity!"

So I can't describe what it was like to wake up to that empty house, that empty bed. There were many days when I didn't want to wake up at all, when I thought that maybe there was a way to just sleep off Adam's death. But Truman changed all that. A puppy has a curious, magical way of boring a hole through despair, chewing up and shredding widow's weeds as if they were nothing more consequential than yesterday's newspaper. Slowly I found myself forced to view the world through Truman's eyes. And what an enchanted world it was, where a simple piece of wadded-up Kleenex held the secret to endless joy, a world in which sadness was unknown unless I created it.

Even the cats seemed to sense that Truman had at least one redeeming virtue. When they heard the familiar, comforting sound of my laughter warming the house like a fire that had been allowed to die out and was now being rekindled, they, too, came creeping back to life. In fact, they even began sleeping in the bed again, right next to Truman.

Of course, this is not an unheard-of phenomenon—pets leading humans through the fog of grief. In a restaurant one day, I struck up a conversation with my waitress. I don't know how we got to talking about life, but we did. She told me that her little brother, the person she was closest to in the world, had died of AIDS. "He was the sweetest person," she said. "You know, he was so weak and all. But he never stopped smiling. He had the greatest smile. Even at the end."

"How did you deal with his death?" I asked.

"Well, I have a very strong faith. And wonderful friends. And I got a dog."

"You did? What kind of dog?"

A Widow, a Chihuahua, and Harry Truman

"Oh, some big mutt. Craziest-looking dog you've ever seen. My kids and I named him Kramer because he reminded us of Kramer on *Seinfeld*. He's got this wild hair that sticks up all over. And he's a real comedian. He does stuff all the time that he knows'll kill us. Like this one time he grabbed a pillow from the couch and put it over his head. Then he peeks out with one eye, you know, to see if he's getting a reaction. We laughed so hard I thought we'd die."

"Oh, I know. After my husband died I never thought I'd ever laugh again. But my puppy, Truman, has me rolling in the aisles."

"Aren't dogs great? Kramer really saved my life."

"Yeah. You know, my husband had the greatest sense of humor. I always have the feeling he brought Truman and me together."

"I bet he did," she said kindly. "I know my brother's cracking up over Kramer."

And that, I'm convinced, is why *God* is *dog* spelled backward.

Chapter 5

Of Time and Puppies

I never worried about whether or not the
decisions I made were popular. I always knew
that time would prove me right.

Harry Truman certainly trusted time more than I did.
In the first months of widowhood, it was my biggest obstacle,
a daily hurdle I was required to jump in order simply to keep
on going.

Everything seemed to be operating in slow motion. I
moved as though in a fog. The hours followed each other in an
endless funeral procession of days and nights. I needed something to help me sleep and something to get me up. The worst
part was opening my eyes to another day without Adam.

We'd had our morning ritual. There was the wake-up kiss,
followed by the very Irish "Good morning, love!" uttered with
the enthusiasm of one who saw *every* morning as good once
he'd found his beloved. There was my coffee, brought in on a
tray and set down on the nightstand as ceremoniously as if I

were Queen Elizabeth. And then Adam would sit at the edge of the bed and we'd talk and joke and plan the day. And before I knew it the morning and afternoon had vanished and it was time for the evening ritual.

Dinner was always an event, because I love to cook and Adam loved to be cooked for (especially after five years as a starving, helpless-in-the-kitchen widower). I'd whip up fabulous meals, candles and all, and we'd eat holding hands, Adam invariably remarking that my food was the best he'd ever tasted, possibly (he conjectured) because it had been prepared with the secret ingredient of love.

After dinner we might work a bit, he on his paintings, I on my writing. At midnight there was *The Twilight Zone*, followed by an old movie, followed by a 3:00 A.M. sandwich in bed and more talking—we never did shut up—until we'd finally hit the hay around 4:00 A.M.

Yes, in those days time seemed to fly. But now, slowed by loneliness, it crawled as though, like me, unable to get back up on its feet. On one particularly torturous day I remembered something a newly widowed man had told me years before, when he was trying to maneuver his way through the shock and numbness of his wife's death from cancer. "People tell me, 'Time is your enemy now, but it will someday become your friend.' They say that time does heal you. But I don't know . . ."

I didn't know either. I was absolutely convinced that I'd be in a state of overwhelming pain for the rest of my life; I couldn't imagine that there was any psychic Krazy Glue strong enough to put me back together again. This attitude, I later discovered, is typical in the early stages of grief. You become quite self-centered, as though your loss is the worst ever experienced by any human being. I wanted to talk about Adam to everyone; I didn't understand why the world still turned and life still went on for others when it had ground to a halt for me. I don't think I exactly wallowed in pain, for it wasn't a place I enjoyed being in. It was more as if I were trapped in quicksand, dragged down against my will into a bubbling pit of desolation.

How wise God and Adam were, then, to saddle me with a puppy.

After years of having cats, who generally don't bother you as long as there's food in their bowl, litter in their box, and an open cat door, I found myself under a daily assault of canine passion that began before I'd opened my eyes. Truman would literally lick me awake; I didn't even have time to remember that I was facing another day of grief. There were now things far more important to be attended to, like tummy rubs, kisses, tickles, and tumbles. My mornings could no longer be spent under the covers, hiding from the world, for there were Truman's basic functions to address. I would stumble out of bed and throw on my clothes at that ungodly hour known as the crack of dawn, vainly inquiring of the gods as to why this dog couldn't use a litter box. When Petie and Rhonda were barely four weeks old, Angel had herded them into the box and toilet-trained them in three minutes flat. But the gods were silent, lips pursed in sphinxlike smugness. "It's your karma," they seemed to be gloating. "After all those carefree years of cat ownership, the party's over. You didn't want children? Ha! You thought a dog would be the easy way out? Ha ha! We've blessed you with a toddler—for the next twenty years! Ha ha ha!"

So, no matter how sleepy or depressed I was, I had to get up and let Truman out. Not only let him out, but follow him around the yard like the gentleman-in-waiting of the infant emperor Pu Yi, encouraging him to answer nature's call and praising him to the skies when he finally did his business.

"*Good* dog!" I would sing, straight out of the puppy training manual, praying like mad that the neighbors weren't at their windows. I felt so stupid that I wanted to put a bag over my head. I tried to imagine degrading myself so completely with the cats and couldn't. Even at four weeks, when they were no more than toddling balls of fur, they probably would have shot me stinging looks of feline contempt. Truman, on the other hand, couldn't have been happier. If you had seen him looking up at me proudly as he squatted, you would have thought he was Andrea Bocelli, performing before an audience of thousands.

And then there are the Embarrassing Things We Do with Our Dogs.

Dog owners have a reputation, not entirely undeserved, of being slightly—shall we be polite?—excessive. Looking back on my pre-Truman days, I remember (quite sheepishly) that I would laugh as hard as anybody at the ludicrous things people do with, to, and for their dogs.

I particularly recall how, some fifteen years ago, I howled along with the rest of the audience at that wonderful documentary *Gates of Heaven,* about pet cemeteries. There was one stand-out, side-splitting sequence of a fat old lady in heavy makeup, big hair, and pointy glasses, teaching her chihuahua to sing. "La la la la la," she screeched; and lo and behold, her little dog chimed right in with a series of excited, high-pitched arfs. The projectionist had to stop the movie because we were all laughing so hysterically that no one could hear the dialogue.

But when, just the other day, I caught myself singing to Truman and trying to make him follow suit, a chill went down my spine. Oh no. It couldn't be. It just *couldn't* be. I was turning into that loony fat lady in *Gates of Heaven*. Soon she and I would be one.

Yes, something happens to you when you become a dog owner. Something insidious creeps into your brain like a fungus and eventually renders you completely insane. And the worst thing is, as with most deadly diseases, you don't realize you've got it until it's too late.

Not that I'd ever consent to become the laughingstock of a movie. But I find myself doing things with Truman that, if discovered, would be far more humiliating to me than being caught in the kinkiest sex act. In fact, I'm not sure why I'm going public with them now. But here they are:

1. Kiss and Cuddle. This is a game we play in the morning, before I've gotten out of bed. Truman starts licking my face and I grab him and kiss him from head to toe, chanting, "Kiss and cuddle! Kiss and cuddle!" Truman immediately goes into an ecstatic state, shoving his nose into my mouth, pawing at my cheek, and finally rolling over, all four legs straight up in the air, whereupon I kiss his stomach, chanting, "Puppy tummy! Puppy tummy! Puppy tummy!"

2. The Puppy Song. From day one I've been singing the following song to Truman:

Truman is a very good dog
A very good dog
A very good dog.
Truman is a very good dog,

A Widow, a Chihuahua, and Harry Truman

The best dog in the world!
[Kiss kiss kiss!]

Truman is a very sweet dog
A very sweet dog
A very sweet dog.
Truman is a very sweet dog,
The sweetest in the world!
[Kiss kiss kiss!]

The verses can, of course, go on indefinitely. Truman loves the Puppy Song; he sits very still, cheek against mine, as I sing it, and he licks me feverishly after each verse. Actually, this song, for which I proudly claim authorship, is a hit on the canine billboard charts; I've sung it to other dogs with great success. In fact, once a great big lab got so excited he began singing it along with me.

3. Photo Display. I became afflicted with photo mania quite early on—actually, only two days into our relationship, when some friends came over on New Year's Day and snapped the first photos of Truman. At three months and three pounds, in his little red turtleneck, he was too adorable to keep a secret. Out would come the photos at the slightest provocation, or sometimes no provocation at all. As the array of photos grew, it wasn't long before all anyone had to do was stand still for me to drag out his picture. And whenever I was around moms taking out photos of their kids, I was right in there, asking if anyone wanted to see a picture of *my* little boy. The fact that mothers of human children didn't respond quite as enthusiastically as I would have liked never deterred me.

The real topper, though, was Truman's passport photo. I dragged him along to the passport photographer when I was preparing for my trip to Ireland, insisting that we be snapped together. Truman was six months old at the time, all turned out in his tiny kitten harness and matching leash.

The photographer, a fat, bored old guy who'd been doing his job for about a hundred years, was jolted out of his terminal apathy by my unexpected request.

"Listen, lady, that's not gonna fly with the authorities. You can't put that dog on your passport photo," he grumped.

"Then just shoot a set for my private collection, okay?"

"It'll cost extra. Fifteen dollars."

Fifteen dollars! A mere pittance to pay for immortality. Unfortunately, Truman was scared by the big camera and the big cameraman, and he looked rather mournful in the photo. In addition, at that age his ears were far bigger than the rest of him, so he somewhat resembled a bat.

Anyway, the passport photo soon became dog-eared, literally and figuratively. I must have shown it to half the globe, including everyone I visited in Ireland and England. My Irish friends good-naturedly tolerated my obsession; and my English friends, being citizens of the ruling country when it comes to eccentricities, animal and otherwise, took out *their* dog photos to show *me*.

4. *The Wheee! Game.* This game developed as a natural outgrowth of tug-of-war with a chihuahua puppy who was hanging on to my sock for dear life. As I tried to extricate it from his mouth, I found myself pulling him along with it, until he suddenly took off, sailing through the air like a kite.

"Wheee!" I exclaimed. He went nuts as soon as he landed, dancing around in circles until he collapsed in dizzy ecstasy.

We played like that from then on, me whirling the sock in the air with Truman attached to it, yelling "Wheee!" like a complete maniac. What a scene in *Gates of Heaven that* would have made.

The Wheee! Game drove Truman so crazy, however, that he became absolutely ferocious. He wouldn't let go of that sock for anything. I could have dragged him half a mile and his little jaws would have remained clamped in an Iron Maiden death grip. This proved to be hazardous to his health: one day, during a particularly frenzied episode, he nearly lost a tooth when I yanked him too hard.

The official Wheee! Game came to an abrupt halt after that. But the word *wheee!* metamorphosed into a general invitation to play. Now when Truman wants to tussle and tumble, he'll dance in front of me invitingly. I yell "Wheee!" and off he goes, leaping up at me and trying to bite my nose. Since I've carefully observed him playing with other dogs, I know just what to do. I swat at him with my paw and growl menacingly, whereupon he screeches to a dead stop and lets me sniff his tummy. Then he rolls over, all four paws in the air, licking my face wildly while I tickle him.

All of this may sound completely revolting to non–dog owners. But one day, when I was rolling on the floor with Truman, convulsed in giggles, it hit me that it was the first time the house had rung with laughter since Adam's death. In fact, Adam was probably chuckling right along with us. I could just see him smiling with indulgent amusement and dubbing us (in one of his favorite Dublin expressions) "a couple of auld eejits."

I lay there and closed my eyes, letting myself be with the laughter, letting it course through me until it rattled my bones and unhinged my brain and swept me away on a current of in-the-moment merriment. Truman danced around me, the cats blinked contentedly, and I laughed until my stomach ached and my body went limp and I fell asleep, right there on the floor.

But it was a good sleep. Not the sleep of escape I was so used to, nor the sleep of death I'd been tempted by, but the sleep of life recharging itself at last.

Chapter 6

Adam's Ashes

I was indeed blessed with luck, to have married
such a good man.

—Bess Truman,
after Harry Truman's funeral

It stood on a shelf, an ungainly black plastic box, too
ugly to display yet too precious to discard. Often I would
look at it and wonder just how and when I was going to deal
with its contents. That box contained my husband's "cremains," and while I knew, logically, that this small pile of ash
and bone wasn't Adam—that he was, as Andrea the psychic
had said, doing just fine in the next world—my human self
was still firmly attached to anything on the physical plane that
had belonged to him. Regardless of where he was now, this
box held the dear body that I had held. Even though that body
had taken another form, how could I let it go?

Ironically, when I'd met Adam, his first wife's ashes were
still in a box on the shelf of *his* closet, five years after her death.
I'd found this strange then, even slightly grotesque. Why was

he keeping such a grisly reminder of her? What purpose did it serve? When I asked him why he hadn't done anything with the ashes, he evaded the issue, mumbling something about just never having gotten around to it. Realizing then that he was still holding on to the last fragile thread of their life together, I didn't press the issue, although from time to time I would gently suggest that he might want to have a small ceremony, maybe with his kids, and scatter Nancy's ashes on the lovely hill that overlooked Santa Paula—a hill she and Adam had both loved.

"That's a good idea," Adam would say, continuing to do nothing. And so, it was his son Tim who finally took the gray cardboard box off the shelf after Adam died. He asked me for a small portion of his father's ashes, and these he scattered, along with his mother's, into the wind, in his own private ceremony in the desert.

As for me, I put the rest of the ashes in the closet, without even realizing that I was doing just what Adam had done, and there they remained until I moved back to Los Angeles, where they promptly took up residence on a new closet shelf.

As the months turned into a year, and then two years, I asked myself why I wasn't dealing with them. Except that I *was*, in my own way. In grief, everything has its own time, its own agenda, and you can't rush the process any more than you can speed up the process of giving birth, or the L.A. Rapid Transit System. The journey out of the thicket of grief and into the pasture of peace isn't a straight road that starts from A and ends at B. Rather, it's a twisted maze, with no guideposts or maps, in which one finds oneself retracing one's steps just when it seems as though headway is at last being made. You can have a truly cheerful moment—a moment, say, when you realize that you haven't cried for a whole day—only to be felled an hour later by some unexpected memory lurking around a corner, lying in wait to trip you up and send you sprawling. In a way, the whole damn seesaw reminded me of a game from my childhood, Chutes and Ladders. In that game, as you may remember, you can be on a roll, hitting so many ladders that you're almost home free, when—*pow!*—you get that dreaded chute at the top and down, down, down you slide, all the way to the starting gate again.

As a matter of fact, not too long ago I played Chutes and Ladders with my six-year-old nephew.

"Oooh!" he groaned, when he landed on a big chute and lost his lead. "How come I had to get that?"

"Because . . . that's life," I said.

He looked at me questioningly.

"This game's a lot like life, Michael," I said, unaware at that moment that my attempt to logically explain the painfully inexplicable was more for my benefit than his. "One minute you're up; the next you're down. You know how you can be roller-skating and having a great time and then suddenly— *ouch!*—you take a tumble and scrape your knees, and then you're crying when you were laughing just a second before?"

He nodded thoughtfully.

"But then you get back up—because you always have to get back up—and soon you're whizzing off again. And maybe you'll fall again and maybe you won't, but it doesn't really matter because it's all part of the game."

"Yup!" he agreed, brightening up. "So I could still beat you, right?" And he rolled the dice, hope rekindled.

Could I still beat the pain of loss, though? Like Death in *The Seventh Seal*, grief seemed to be my grimly clever adversary, determined to dog my heels until I finally surrendered to the pain and died of a broken heart. And, like the knight who enters into a battle of wits with Death in that movie, I had only the weapon of my own ingenuity. There's only one problem with this theory: it's impossible to outwit grief. As long as you regard it as your enemy, you'll never learn what it has to teach you.

After Adam died, my therapist gave me the following poem by her favorite poet, Sylvia Townsend Warner. It's called "Azrael," which in Hebrew means the Angel of Death, and it beautifully sums up the process of resigning oneself to loss.

AZRAEL

Who chooses the music, turns the page,
Waters the geraniums on the window ledge?
Who proxies my hand,
Puts on the mourning ring in lieu of the diamond?

Who winds the trudging clock, who tears
Flimsy the empty date off calendars?
Who widow-hoods my senses
Lest they should meet the morning's cheat
defenceless?

Who valets me at nightfall, undresses me of another day,
Puts it tidily and finally away,
And lets in darkness
To befriend my eyelids like an illusory caress?

I called him Sorrow when first he came,
But Sorrow is too narrow a name;

A Widow, a Chihuahua, and Harry Truman

And though he has attended me all this long while
Habit will not do. Habit is servile,
He, inaudible, governs my days, impalpable,
Impels my hither and thither. I am his to command,
My times are in his hand.
Once in a dream I called him Azrael.

It wasn't until perhaps two years after Adam's death, when life had once again become something to look forward to rather than something to dread, that I truly understood the powerful meaning of this poem. Looking back, I can now see grief not as my adversary but as a stern and compassionate companion, who remains with you even as you try to run from him. He knows that all you're really doing is running in place, and that eventually you'll be forced to drop from sheer exhaustion, until he holds out his arms and you fall into them, into the terrifying abyss of seemingly bottomless pain that, in the oddest way, eventually turns out to be your salvation.

Today I can't believe that I'm so much stronger, so much more open and compassionate, so much less afraid of both living and dying than I was before Adam's death. Surrendering yourself to grief will do that for you, if you let it. Through that process, I found inner resources I hadn't known I had. I learned how to survive after my soul had been torn open, my heart shattered. And most important, I learned *why*—why I was supposed to keep going, why life is too precious to be disowned, even in the midst of unbearable pain.

A lot of this growth has to do with a sense of purpose, or, as the great psychoanalyst and concentration camp survivor Viktor Frankl put it, "man's search for meaning." When we feel that we're part of a larger picture, that there's a reason for our being around, a special contribution that we alone can make, we're much better able to live with and rise above pain. A lot of it has to do with your own "mattering"—how much you mean to others, how selfish it would be for you to check out when there are still people who love and need you. And a lot of it has to do with love itself—how we as human beings naturally go in search of love to heal us and give us new life.

When I lost Adam, I felt as though I had lost love forever. Who else could ever know me so well; who else would ever be willing to dig deep into me and cherish everything he un-earthed, flaws as well as virtues? Yet even though I couldn't conceive of another relationship or another husband, I still needed love—in fact, needed it more than ever. And even though I didn't realize it at the time, Truman was more than just a means of distracting myself from grief. The act of getting him was actually an act of recommitting myself to life, a sign of the willingness to love and be loved again.

With Adam I was inordinately fortunate to have been given the all-too-rare experience of unconditional love. I never felt that I had to change in any way for him; I knew that he adored me simply for who I was, not for what he hoped I could become.

And the love I felt for him was the same. I'll never forget the summer afternoon when Adam was in the throes of chemo and seemed to have aged thirty years in six weeks. As we lay in bed, holding each other and resting, he said to me, "How can you still love me, the way I look?"

I gazed at his emaciated face, his bald head, his shrunken body. Incredibly enough, he had never looked more beautiful to me. I suddenly realized that as his physical self was disappear-ing, his soul was expanding, burning more and more brightly until its light seemed to fill the whole room. And at that magic moment, I was seized with an overwhelming sense of peace. I actually felt the tangible union with another's soul that would endure forever, beyond death.

After Adam died, I turned to food for solace, drugging myself with bad things like pizza and macaroni and cheese, foods that would calm me, numb me, and put me into a drowsy stupor. Naturally I gained forty pounds in a very short period of time—forty pounds that kept me from considering even the possibility of a new relationship, forty pounds that became my protective shield against a world that seemed, at that moment, so capriciously cruel.

I had been overweight when I met Adam, but that didn't cool his ardor in the least. In fact, after we became lovers he dragged out all his Rubens art books for inspiration and began painting me in the nude, turning what I felt were ugly rolls of extra flesh into veritable visions of voluptuous beauty. "I love every inch of you," he would exclaim. And the most amazing thing was that he really meant it.

I don't know if I'll ever meet another man who could love me that way. But I've met a dog. It wouldn't matter to Truman if I weighed a ton; his love is as pure and unconditional as was Adam's, and the way he throws himself at me when I come in the door, or licks me in a furious game of Kiss and Cuddle, is reminiscent of the way Adam would grab me and hold me tight when I returned after a day away, or cuddle with me in bed, kissing and giggling far into the wee hours. As Adam did, Truman drinks in love like a sponge; there's no such thing as too much of it. The cats have their limits; they want only so much petting before some sort of imaginary bell goes off and they struggle to extricate themselves from my embrace. But I have yet to discover Truman's love saturation point, any more than I could discover Adam's. The more we loved each other, the more we loved each other.

Maybe that's another reason I so like Harry Truman: that's how he felt about his Bess. From the age of approximately six, when he first met Elizabeth Wallace at Sunday school, until his death at eighty-eight, he was hopelessly in love with her, and there are some three thousand letters to prove it. Letters he wrote to her from his farm when they were courting and limited to Sunday meetings ("I wish every day were Sunday. Do you suppose it will ever be?"); from the front during WWI when they were engaged ("I'm crazy about you. . . . All I ask is love me always and if I have to be shot I'll try and not have it in the back or before a stone wall because I'm afraid not to do you honor"); from the U.S. Senate ("I think my sweetheart is better looking today if that is possible, and you know it is not fashionable now to think that of the same one . . ."); from the White House ("You are still on the pedestal where I placed you that day in Sunday school 1890. What an old fool I am"); from his postpresidency travels ("You're the nicest sweetheart a man could have. From your no account partner, who loves you more than ever")—letters that, even sixty-five years after Bess and Harry met, still brimmed with pure, unadulterated adoration. It was a well-known, if knock-me-down-dead unbelievable, fact that in a town, a profession, and a world where infidelity was the norm, Harry Truman had been faithful to Bess all his life, and had not, in fact, so much as glanced at another woman since that fateful "Sunday school 1890" day.

Adam was that way too. A one-woman man, the kind a wife doesn't have to worry about and, if she's smart, treasures like the most priceless jewel. I may be old-fashioned, but I think that's the kind of guy all women dream of down deep. Bess Truman and I were lucky that way—very, very lucky.

What would Harry Truman have done with Bess's ashes, I wondered, had he had the misfortune to outlive her? Banished them to a musty closet shelf, where the light never shone and secrets went to die a lonely, unrevealed death? Relinquished them to the wind or the sea, great but impersonal powers that, never having known the woman he loved, could not necessarily be trusted to treat her gently? Kept them on the mantel in a large urn befitting her large presence, as though the tough, big-busted woman who had ruled his heart for eighty years were there still, presiding with stern, loving authority over his remaining days?

Of course, the bottom line was, what did it matter what Harry Truman might have done with Bess's ashes? This was *my* issue, *my* challenge, to be resolved deep within myself. Grief, as I'm sure Harry would have informed me in no uncertain terms, is a very private matter, nobody else's goddamn business. You do what feels right, when it feels right, and that's all there is to it.

A day finally did come when I made my peace with Adam's ashes and realized that letting go didn't mean giving up.

But meanwhile the black box stayed where it was, wedged in between Adam's old hat and a box of Christmas ornaments, patiently waiting for its destiny to be decided.

Chapter 7

Truman's Treasure Pile

I always admired a plaque I once saw, "MAKE NO LITTLE
PLANS." I don't believe in little plans. You can always
amend a big plan but you can never expand a little one.

Truman shared Harry Truman's belief in the importance
of planning big. If I was the queen of procrastination, he was
the king of action. As with his namesake, there didn't seem to
be a thing for which he didn't immediately have a plan—the
bigger the better.

Almost as soon as he arrived at his new home, he began
running off with anything that wasn't nailed down. In fact, his
favorite activity seemed to be accumulating and hoarding con-
traband. His treasure pile, which was usually located in the
middle of the living room, contained all sorts of interesting
loot, from his various toys and scraps of paper to shoes, wal-
lets, books, underwear—you name it. If he'd been in charge of
Adam's ashes, they would have found their permanent home
in his treasure pile in the flick of a whisker.

A Widow, a Chihuahua, and Harry Truman

Many was the time I'd see him trotting busily by my office door with some huge prize—often something bigger than he—clenched firmly in his little mouth. One day he dragged a boot over to the treasure pile; on another occasion I found half of the manuscript of my latest book carefully strewn among pig ears and rubber bones. And then there was the famous morning I couldn't find my four-hundred-dollar glasses. I groped around the house blindly until I thought of his treasure pile. Sure enough, there they were. He'd chewed only one of the lenses, thank God.

One day a postcard came from the vet. Addressed to Truman Shields, it reminded us that it was time to go in for a rabies shot. Guess who was on the twenty-cent stamp? Yes, sir: Harry S. Truman. I got so excited that I grabbed Truman and waved the postcard in his face. "Look! There he is, the man you were named after! On a postcard addressed to you!" Truman stared at me and Harry. Then he grabbed the postcard in his teeth and ran off with it. It ended up in his treasure pile, amidst the underwear and old Kleenex, like some sort of doggie shrine to our thirty-third president.

Since the cats had never exhibited any such larcenous inclinations, Truman's stash was always a bit of an amazement to me. What pleasure could he possibly find in stockpiling wads of Kleenex or socks or old bottle caps? But I was rapidly learning that when it comes to dogs, ours is not to reason why. It became evident from day one that while the cats were basically interested only in eating and sleeping, Truman had An Agenda. There were things he needed to do, places he needed to go, people he needed to see. What, where, who, and particularly why, I hadn't the faintest clue. But his small brain was busy, that was for sure.

And busier than we might think. One night I came home late to find one of the most amazing things I've ever seen—second only to the *Apollo* moon landing and my grandmother's whalebone corset. In the middle of the living-room floor was the big electric blanket from my king-size bed. At first I couldn't believe what I was seeing. Then my brain grew fuzzy trying to compute the incredible data. Either Truman or an alien had done this. I had heard of aliens abducting *people,* but never, to my knowledge, *blankets.* Thus one had to conclude that a four-pound puppy had managed to get an object approximately three times his weight and thirty-six times his size (a) off the bed, (b) out of the bedroom, (c) through the hallway, and (d) into the living room. This would have been the equivalent of me dragging a 450-pound, 210-square-foot something a distance of a city block—in my teeth.

Truman had obviously not only made a Big Plan; he'd carried it out. Naturally, he looked justifiably proud as he surveyed his biggest kill to date. I should have had the blanket mounted on the wall, like one of those hunter's or fisherman's trophies. What mystified me even more than the act itself was the strategizing it took, not to mention the determination. It was one of those strange things high on his Agenda. One of those things that define a dog's entire life, imbuing it with meaning and purpose, however meaningless and purposeless it might seem to us.

I gathered up the blanket. Because it was too awkward to carry, I dragged it back into the bedroom. I looked down at Truman and wanted to ask, "How . . . ?" He looked up at me anxiously, bewildered as to why I would be absconding with his bounty. It occurred to me that we were both somewhat in the same boat, forever doomed to ponder the unanswerable.

I put the blanket back on the bed. "This," I said sternly to Truman, "belongs on the bed and not on the floor."

Truman whimpered a little. I picked him up and kissed him. "You performed a magnificent feat tonight," I said. "You are a wonder dog."

Truman licked me excitedly. Later I checked the chihuahua book but could find no mention of What to Do When Your Puppy Steals Your Electric Blanket. This was obviously an original, Truman-created act that belonged not in a dog manual but in the *Guinness Book of World Records.*

You just may find it there someday.

Chapter 8

Angel's Ashes

I get angry like anybody else. But I don't
stay angry. Being bitter . . . that's for people
who aren't busy with other matters.

Having an outstandingly practical nature, Harry Truman
might have been too busy with more important matters to
waste valuable time and energy on anger. But for me, anger
was one of the scariest, and yet most legitimate, phases of
grief. You'd think that after someone you love dies, it would
make you feel better to concentrate on the good memories, to
take everybody's well-meaning advice and "be thankful for
the wonderful relationship you had." But although you may
sincerely *want* to be thankful, you can't help being angry.
Damn angry. Angry that your beloved has been taken from
you, angry that you had only four years together, angry that
he had to suffer so terribly, angry that other people have each
other and you're all alone. Oh, the list of grievances against

God can be endless. Down deep you feel terrible—ungrateful and mean-spirited. But let me tell you, there isn't a thing you can do about it except accept it. It isn't until you can let the anger out (in ways not destructive to you or others), let it run its course, that you can move toward a more rational, balanced existence.

Sometimes I'd get so angry I'd scare myself. The least little thing could set me off: a bottle cap that wouldn't open, a pair of socks I couldn't find might be all it took to send me into orbit. I'd march around the house emitting a stream of expletives until I collapsed in tears and cried myself into merciful exhaustion. I know that this was good for me; if I hadn't unleashed my terrible rage, which was really pain crying out for attention, it undoubtedly would have poisoned my system, resulting in serious illness.

But I didn't realize what a profoundly unsettling effect my outbursts might have on the animals.

Rhonda and Petie would bolt out their cat door at the first puff of smoke from Mount Vesuvius. They knew enough to give me space, returning some hours later when they sensed that the coast was clear. But poor little Truman would hide under the coffee table or the chair or the bed, shaking in terror and refusing to come out even after I'd calmed down. No matter how sweetly I wheedled and coaxed him, he remained wary and sad for some time, huddled in a defiant little ball, tail between his legs, ears drooping.

You can never know the real meaning of one-hundred-percent certified guilt until you look into the frightened eyes of a child or an animal and know that you have been the cause of its terror. No matter that you had no intention of causing hurt; your ego-centered actions have had a terrible, perhaps permanent, effect on a helpless creature. Yes, that was all I needed, a nice, big load of guilt to add on to the back-breaking burden of grief I was carting around. I felt helpless. At the same time, I couldn't help but be impressed by the fascinating fact that human beings are the only species on earth who have anger in their emotional repertoire.

When you think about it, anger is unknown in the animal world. Oh, animals may *seem* angry when they bare their teeth or attack another animal. But their actions are motivated not by anger but by fear, not by feelings of self-pity or indignation but by an overriding instinct for self-preservation or protection of their young. Yeah, I know, sometimes your cat or dog might act pissed off with you if you leave him or her alone all day or have the nerve to take a vacation. But that's pretty mild compared to the anger that causes human beings to do terrible things to other human beings or to themselves.

So, while I knew, logically, that I was entitled to have a temper tantrum in the privacy of my own home, I realized that other sentient beings living with me were being adversely affected by my moods. Somehow I had to figure out a way to let my anger out while at the same time protecting the faithful companions who depended on me for emotional as well as physical security.

Even in grief, I learned, one has to be respectful of others. So, I tried to have my little outbursts in the car, or to be quieter about them. Sometimes it worked and sometimes it didn't. But in the process I think I became a little less self-centered, and a little more appreciative of the fact that the animals were grieving too and needed my support as much as I needed theirs.

Gradually the rage began to dissipate. As the months passed, I found myself wanting to be less angry and more in touch with

A Widow, a Chihuahua, and Harry Truman

the lovely memories of my marriage that until now had been too painful to revisit.

So, on a balmy spring morning some eight months after Adam's death, when new life was in the air and the world seemed to be shaking off its winter lethargy (there is such a thing even in California), I awoke feeling brave enough to confront certain feelings I'd been avoiding—the feelings of love and joy and contentment and gratitude that I had felt for Adam with my marriage and that I had allowed to be eclipsed by anger and rage.

I decided to spend a couple of days at what had been our favorite hotel in San Luis Obispo, four hours north of Santa Paula. If I went back to that hotel, I thought, perhaps those feelings would come flooding back. Perhaps I'd even be lucky enough to get caught in one of those *Twilight Zone* time warps where you suddenly become young again and lost joy is recaptured in a miracle that defies time, space, and death.

I made reservations at the Apple Farm, a beautiful inn that had a fireplace in every room, a running stream, and an old mill, and I arranged for someone to come in and feed the cats.

As for Truman, however, I was faced with the dubious prospect of putting him in a kennel. Fortunately my vet had one she highly recommended. It was run by a short, tough, gravelly voiced woman in her seventies named Madeleine, whose specialty was chihuahuas. In fact, her particular claim to fame was her own chihuahua, Radar, who had won first prize in the Small Breed category at Westminster, an ultraprestigious affair that is to dog shows what Wimbledon is to tennis, or the Vatican is to the Catholic Church.

As I loaded Truman into the car with his toys, I felt as shaky as a new mother on her kid's first day of school. I don't know whose separation anxiety was worse, Truman's or mine. He was only seven months old, after all, and we'd never been apart. How would he survive?

"Aw, he'll be fine!" croaked Madeleine, when we were all introduced. "My, you're a big fella, aren't ya?" she clucked, stroking Truman, who was so excited he didn't know who to pee on first—Madeleine, her daughter Brenda, or the resident cat, Shingles, a four-footed member of the welcoming committee who was as cordial to Truman as his nasty cat brother and sisters would never dream of being.

We settled Truman into his quarters, which consisted of a big outdoor pen connected via "hallway" to an indoor cage where he would sleep, safely away from the cold. I produced the overnight items Madeleine had told me to bring—Truman's favorite toy, a black-and-white stuffed cat that looked just like Petie and that he dragged all over the house, a couple of tinkly bones, his sweater, and a shirt of mine so that he'd have my scent to reassure him.

"He'll have a good old time," Madeleine assured me, as Truman immediately ran to the chain-link fence to sniff the little Yorkie on the other side.

"What about his meals?" I inquired nervously. "He's a really picky eater."

"Not here he won't be," barked Madeleine. "They get fed twice a day. Science Diet. They have five minutes to eat, and if they haven't finished by then, too bad. We take away the bowls. It doesn't take very long for them to fall in line, I can tell you. But don't worry," she added, seeing my consternation. "They've always got their kibble to fall back on."

I gulped. Was this summer camp or boot camp?

"We don't spoil 'em here," Madeleine went on. "But we

A Widow, a Chihuahua, and Harry Truman

love 'em. Aw, take it easy," she said kindly, as the dreaded moment of parting approached and I gathered Truman up for one last kiss. "It's always tough, that first time away. Now as you leave, don't look back. You'll be tempted to. But just walk away fast. It's better that way, for both of you."

On the way out, Madeleine introduced me to the resident celebrity, Radar, whose pen was on the other side of Truman's and whose photo, with his trophy at Westminster, was mounted proudly on the wall of her office.

"Full-blooded champion," she bragged. "Of course, that was ten years ago, when he was a young man."

It sure was. Radar was now a grizzly bearded, fat old thing. He creaked and grunted and I could just hear him regaling his suitemates with his youthful triumphs ("Did I ever tell ya about the time I won Westminster?") while they yawned and rolled their eyes and groaned, "Oh, God, here we go again."

"Now remember," said Madeleine. "No looking back."

I started down the walk toward the car. But I couldn't resist taking one last look at my baby. Fully expecting to be turned into a pillar of salt, I glanced over my shoulder.

Truman was gripping the door to his pen, watching me and whimpering. One ear was drooping, and the look on his face was so pitiful that I almost ran back and grabbed him. But then I realized that Madeleine was right. There comes a time in every mother's life when she has to trust her child to make it in the big, cruel world without her twenty-four-hour-a-day guiding hand.

As I got in the car I realized, to my surprise, that I was crying. He's only a dog, for Christ's sake, I scolded myself. You're leaving him for two days, not two years. Yet I knew that I was crying for more than met the eye. It had been only eight months since death had forced me to confront the agony of permanent separation, and so being away from a creature I loved, even for a brief period, hit a nerve that was still painfully exposed. I blew my nose and drove off, but I knew that the image of that forlorn little face, with the drooping ear and frightened eyes, would be burned into my memory forever. How the hell, I wondered, do parents ever get away and manage to enjoy themselves?

Little did I know that I was in for a far more devastating parting.

The following morning, as I got up to pack for my little getaway, I noticed a highly unusual sight: Angel. She was sitting on the bedroom floor, by the door.

Since she pretty much lived outside now, I was pleasantly surprised. "Angel, honey!" I exclaimed. "What are you doing here?"

But when she turned to me, I cried out.

Her entire jaw was torn off and hanging by a thread. Her head was swollen and one of her dazed eyes was filled with blood.

The sight was so horrible that I turned away. I grabbed the phone book to find the nearest pet emergency clinic; it was Sunday and my vet's office would be closed. But my hands were shaking so violently that I couldn't even turn the pages.

The nearest emergency room was ten miles away. I called, and they said to bring her in as soon as I could. It took all the courage I had to pick Angel up, mangled face and all. But I grabbed her and rushed her into the van, not even stopping to put her in her carrier.

That was a mistake I'll regret for the rest of my days. After getting her settled in the front passenger seat, I reached down to set my purse on the floor. This gave Angel just enough time to jump out the open door and run off.

I couldn't imagine how she could even move. But as I ran after her, calling her, she disappeared into the thicket behind our house.

"Oh, my God," I sobbed. "Angel, please. *Please* come out."

But she was gone. Crying disconsolately, I continued calling her until I collapsed on the ground with a distress-induced asthma attack that required medication. A friend came over to be with me and calm me, but I was hopelessly distraught. Finally I managed to reach my vet on her pager.

"There's nothing you can do," she said flatly. "This is an animal. She's operating purely on instinct, and instinct tells animals to crawl into a bush or a hole when they know they're going to die."

"You don't think she'll come back?"

"She might. But there's no guarantee."

I told her that I had plans to take off that afternoon for a weekend getaway, and that it was too late to cancel the reservations at the hotel.

"You need to get away," she said. "Don't ruin your weekend. Whoever is feeding the other cats can look out for Angel, and if she comes back, they can get her to emergency and call you."

I waited until five o'clock that afternoon. When Angel still hadn't returned, I called the sitter and left detailed instructions with her. If Angel came back, she was to take her to the Ventura Pet Emergency Clinic and call me, and I'd come back immediately. I even gave her my credit card number, to pay for any medical procedures. Then I left, with an army of misgivings and a heart as heavy as a boulder.

Between calling my sitter every few hours to check on Angel, and calling Madeleine's to check on Truman, the weekend was a fiasco. I had purposely reserved one of the rooms at the Apple Farm that Adam had particularly loved, and as I lay there in the big canopy bed where we'd once made wild love, I was filled with such desolation that I couldn't even weep.

"Oh, Adam," I whispered. "Can't you find Angel and send her back? She loved you so much."

I decided to leave earlier than planned. When I returned home, I went into the backyard and called Angel again and again. But the only answer I got was the rustling of the leaves and the sighing of the wind. Sadly, I sat down at the computer and worked for awhile. Then I went into the bedroom. And there, on the floor, was Angel.

She turned to look at me. Her head was now the size of a softball and her jaw had completely fallen off, giving her a grinning, skeletal appearance. The odor of necrotizing flesh made my stomach turn. She had lost so much weight in less than forty-eight hours that she looked almost like a kitten again. But she was still alive. And she'd dragged herself in at the sound of my voice.

When I picked her up, she offered no resistance. This time I put her in the carrier and raced her to my vet.

"Poor baby," Dr. Blanton whispered, shaking her head.

"What happened to her?" I asked. "It looks as though she was in a fight with a possum or a coyote."

"No. I'd say she was hit by a car." Dr. Blanton looked at me compassionately.

"I know this is going to be awfully hard for you. But we have to put her to sleep."

I nodded, breaking down in tears.

A Widow, a Chihuahua, and Harry Truman

"I know you lost your husband not long ago." She handed me a Kleenex. "My heart goes out to you. But this is the most merciful thing we can do at this point."

"If only I hadn't left," I sobbed. "If only I'd canceled the weekend. Maybe she would have come back sooner."

"Please don't do that to yourself," Dr. Blanton said gently. "She did what she had to do; you did what you had to do. I would never have recommended that you cancel your plans. Besides, you couldn't have saved her; her injuries were too severe."

I stroked Angel's swollen forehead and she looked up at me gratefully. Her eyes were already growing dim.

"Do you want to hold her while I give her the injection?"

I nodded and gathered Angel up into my arms. Memories came rushing back, of the tiny, scrappy kitten I'd rescued at the pet store, of the day she rode on Snicky's back, of the five kittens she'd nursed so lovingly, of Adam's proud grin as she lay in his lap purring up at him. And then memories of Adam's eyes as they glazed over with approaching death, just like Angel's, and of the terrible moment when the eyes rolled back and the body grew still and I was plunged into the icy waters of widowhood.

Dr. Blanton administered the injection. Angel sighed, closed her eyes, and went limp. Mercifully, it seemed as though she had simply gone to sleep. I continued to hold her and cry, and Dr. Blanton gave me the box of Kleenex. She asked if I wanted to have Angel cremated, and I said yes. She said it would take about a week for them to send me the ashes. And then she said that since Angel had loved Adam so much, the two of them were probably together now, and would never be separated again.

The following morning I went to pick Truman up. When he saw me he went crazy, spinning around like a top and yelping with joy.

"He enjoyed himself," Madeleine said. "He ate all his food, and he played with us and developed quite a nice little relationship with Boomer, here." She motioned to the little Yorkie next door to Truman. "Oh, Boomer, it's okay," she said, as the Yorkie whined plaintively. "Truman'll be back soon."

When we got into the car, I held Truman tightly.

"Truman," I said. "Something very sad happened this weekend."

Truman looked up at me quizzically.

"Angel died, honey. She was hit by a car and we had to put her to sleep."

Now I don't know whether it was just the sadness in my voice, or whether this tiny little puppy understood what I was saying. But what he did next stunned me.

He hung his head. And then he put his front paws over his eyes.

"Oh, sweetheart," I whispered. "It's okay."

He crawled into my lap and kept his head hidden beneath my arm the whole way home. When we got into the house, he wasn't his usual electrically charged self. Instead, he sniffed around, as if looking for Angel. Then he curled up on the couch and looked at me sadly.

The following week I went to pick up Angel's ashes. They were in a much nicer container than Adam's, a pretty, round, silver-and-white tin that looked as if it might have held Christmas cookies. Inside was a card that read, in beautifully flowing script, "In Remembrance of Angel, April 29, 1997."

I put Angel's ashes where they belonged, next to Adam's on the closet shelf. When it came time, I would scatter them together. But for now, the two boxes stood side by side, and I couldn't help thinking that Angel was finally at rest, reunited at last with the person that she, like me, had loved most in the world.

Chapter 9

Truman's House

This place is a tomb without you and your mother.

—From a letter to Margaret Truman,
written from the White House

When Adam died, I realized that I had lost not only my dearest companion; I had lost my home as well.

Oh, I still had the house. But the special, alchemical magic of our love, which had transformed the house into a home, was gone. This cozy little adobe-style structure had been so many things to us—our love nest, our refuge, the silent witness to the greatest joy we had ever known, and the greatest sorrow. The room in which we had first made love was also the room where Adam died, in a small hospital bed that had no room for me. I would sit next to him, holding his thin hand through the handrails, until, overtaken by weariness, I would stumble into the spare bedroom and try to catch an hour or two of sleep. But like a new mother, I always kept one eye open, one ear cocked. I'd check on him every few hours during the night, which was far longer for him than it was for me. His face would light up with joy and relief when I came in, and although he never once throughout his entire illness complained, instead accepting his lot with a great, quiet courage that astounded me, he would invariably whisper, "I missed you awfully last night."

Often, after his death, I would sleep in that room, just so I could share the last space that had held his essence. It might seem morbid to some, but I felt oddly comforted, close to him. Sometimes it seemed as though he hadn't died at all, and that he'd be coming back soon, like a traveler returning from strange and distant lands, full of stories about his adventures. Other times the awful memory of his death, of the last kiss he tried to blow me in spite of his struggle to breathe, would hit me like a savage left hook to the soul, knocking me back into desolate reality. Eventually I came to realize that I was becoming a prisoner of my dreams, a wanderer on a groundless path, my footsteps disappearing in the fine dust of memory.

It wasn't a particularly productive way to live, but it was the only way I knew. I spent about six months in this bittersweet limbo, until I finally realized that it was time for me to move back to Los Angeles and restart my life. So, reluctantly, I put the house on the market.

My Realtor, a sweet, perky woman named Cynthia, assured me that the whole process would be easy as pie. Realtors would always give me twenty-four-hour advance notice before invading the premises. The house would sell quickly, she was sure. But Cynthia hadn't factored in the seemingly inconsequential detail of a chihuahua puppy.

Oh, she knew about Truman; she'd even witnessed a performance of our special game, totally falling to pieces when his ears shot up like guided missiles at the invitation, "Truman! Want to play the Wheee Game?"

"Oh, my Lord. He knows what you're saying!" Cynthia was obviously impressed. "Look at his little ears!"

It got even better when Truman saw the sock and began dancing wildly in a circle.

"I'm going to die!" Cynthia gasped, the tears streaming down her cheeks as I yelled "Wheee!" and Truman dove for the sock, rising in the air like a helium balloon.

Soon, word of the most adorable chihuahua you've ever seen made the rounds of the realty offices. And Truman didn't disappoint; whenever a Realtor showed up with a prospective buyer, he would greet them ecstatically at the door, as if they'd come just to visit him.

"So *this* is Truman," they'd exclaim, and he'd paw their shins and lick them madly, as though they were his dearest long-lost relatives.

But if Truman's charm spelled Realtor heaven, his other habits spelled Realtor hell.

In my innocent pre-canine days I had entertained the idea of getting a chihuahua only because they were the smallest thing one could legally and morally classify as a dog. How much, for instance, could they eat? And how much damage could they do? They couldn't fly through the air and pull the curtains down in one fell swoop, like the cats. They weren't big enough to get into major mischief, like my cousin's golden retriever puppy, who, bored with his regular culinary fare, ate chunks of her new custom-made leather couch one day when she was at work.

No, a chihuahua's influence seemed limited by the laws of nature and mathematics to a border region between earth and sky of no more than two feet. In other words, if you kept stuff off the floor and the coffee table, you should be safe, right?

So much for mathematics. It became evident all too soon that what a chihuahua lacks in size, it makes up for in atomic energy. I personally have never seen anything so small destroy so much in so little time. Once while I was in the shower, Truman shredded the binding of a book. When I went to sleep one night I had a nice bathroom rug; when I awoke the next morning I had a bald rug and a bathroom full of green fluff. Truman gnawed through furniture legs with the speed and intensity of a beaver, and he had a particular taste for pencils, demolishing them in minutes and leaving just the stub as a triumphant calling card. I thought he'd die of lead poisoning, but the vet just laughed. He's a puppy; he'll live. The question was, would I?

Unfortunately, I wasn't thinking ahead when it came to showing the house. Now as anyone who's ever tried to sell a house knows, the twenty-four-hour notice thing is a pack of bull. I can't count the times I got calls from crafty Realtors who were "just down the street" and couldn't they please pop in briefly with their client, who probably would never, ever be in town again in my lifetime?

Not wanting to lose any prospects, I would say yes and frantically start cleaning, while Truman would follow behind me, just as frantically destroying my work. One time when I had about fifteen minutes to straighten up, Truman, unbeknownst to me, had opened up the cupboard under the bathroom sink and gotten into a box of tampons. Because I just had time to whirl through the premises before the doorbell rang, I had no idea that Truman was retracing my steps and leaving his mark in the rooms I had just left. Imagine my horror when the Realtor—a particularly prim and spiffy older woman—began leading her clients on a tour of the bedrooms, only to find tampons all over the floor, taken out of their wrappers and completely dismantled, like bombs that had been carefully disarmed. Truman ran in, chest puffed out with pride, beaming at all of us as if he'd done something wonderful.

I have to hand it to the Realtor. All she said was, "Well. I see this is *Truman*'s house."

One night when I was vacuuming like crazy, one step ahead of another Realtor who had called five minutes before, Truman got into Rhonda and Petie's bag of catnip and spread it all over the carpet like lawn seed—just as the doorbell rang, of course.

"What is *that?*" inquired Isaac, the Realtor, staring down at the strange mess.

"Uh, catnip. The dog . . ." I mumbled helplessly. "I'd just vacuumed . . ."

"It's okay," said Isaac. He was one of those totally cool Realtors who probably should have been a Zen monk. "Don't clean it up. It adds character."

On the day Truman dragged my underwear out for all the Realtors and their clients to admire, I e-mailed my cousin Claire in frustration—the same cousin whose golden retriever, Casey, had eaten the couch. She sent me the following reassuring response:

Dear Cuz,

Don't I know what you're going through! My Realtor held a big open house when my house went on the market, for all the hotshot Realtors in my area. I was traveling at the time, but she was familiar with the dogs and knew how to handle them, so I wasn't worried. Well, in the middle of not only this big open house but a lunch that she had catered at my home for these top-billing Realtors, she tells me that Miss Cider and Mr. Casey wandered off to Mommy's laundry basket and proceeded to remove her underwear and bras and prance around the house in front of all these Realtors with the undergarments in their mouths, at which point I'm sure the dogs started playing tug-of-war with one of the bras (since that's what always happens). My Realtor said, "Claire, knowing you, I just thought you would have died!" Yes, I did.

Nonetheless, Truman charmed every Realtor who came through, even Wanda Brynkowski. Wanda was an Eastern European émigré who was probably a perfectly acceptable human being in the eyes of God and her husband and children. In *my* eyes, however, she was the Realtor from Hell. She was pushy and whiny and never, ever gave me twenty-four-hour notice. In fact, she hardly ever called at all. Instead, she'd just show up at my door, clients in tow, and try to whine her way in.

"Please, is short notice, I know . . ."

"Short notice? Wanda, is *no* notice!"

"Okay, yes. But my clients are here, and we are just in the neighborhood . . ."

Sometimes I'd give in. But other times I'd stand my ground on sheer principle and refuse to let her in. Then she'd invariably resort to her next tactic: fibbing.

"But I call and call yesterday and there is no answer. I *try* to give notice."

"I never got a message from you."

"I think maybe your machine is not on."

"Wanda, did you forget?" I'd look her straight in the eye. "We live in the age of voice-mail. My voice-mail is *always* on."

Then we'd have a stare-down, with her giving me a pathetic look that said, basically, "Okay. I'm a liar. What else is new?"

Eventually I'd let her in, only because she was the squatter type and it probably would have taken the National Guard to remove her from my property.

In addition, Wanda, as you might expect, was given to hyperbole. Whenever she dragged someone through, she'd deliver such a hyped-up pitch that you would have thought we were at Versailles. "You are going to *love* it!" she would gush. "Is gorgeous! Spacious! Magnificent! Your dream home!"

Thus it is with particular relish that I recall the day Wanda got her comeuppance. During one of her grandiose tours she stepped smack in the middle of a pile of Truman's you-know-what, which had been so well camouflaged on a dark-brown area of the carpet that I hadn't noticed it.

"Thees is dog poop!" she announced in a horrified tone.

"It sure is," I agreed pleasantly.

"How do you expect to sell house with dog poop on floor?"

"Well, you never know, Wanda. People have the *strangest* tastes . . ."

"You are bad boy," Wanda scolded Truman, who fixed her with his most beguiling look. "You make bad mess!"

But Truman merely jumped up and started pawing Wanda's leg, his tail whirring like a little propeller. Eventually, because she was not *all* bad, Wanda bent down and picked him up.

"I have two big dogs and they *never* do bad things," she lectured Truman, who responded by licking her nose. Well, that was it. Even Dragon Lady caved in.

"Oh, he is so adorable!" she sighed. "Maybe if you say he

comes along with property, we will sell house, bang! Just like that."

Wanda was probably right; if Truman's face had been on the listing, there probably would have been a bidding war. As it was, after seven long months we finally had an offer we couldn't refuse.

Was it a coincidence that escrow closed on August 5, the day I had met Adam and the first day I had ever set foot in the house?

And so, my life in Santa Paula having come full circle, I loaded the cats and Truman in the car, squared my shoulders, and prepared to start all over again.

Chapter 10

New Friends

A president has to be willing, indeed anxious, to
talk to people. You'll find that the willingness to talk
to people is true of all the great men in our history.

If there's one great thing about dogs, it's how they absolutely force you to meet your neighbors.

I had found a wonderful house in L.A. to rent, high on a hill in a secluded neighborhood. It was paradise: a panoramic view of the city and the mountains, a Jacuzzi and sauna, a huge master bedroom—who could ask for anything more?

It was missing one thing, of course: Adam. At night, standing on my balcony and looking out at the twinkling lights that adorned the landscape like a carpet of jewels, I ached inside. All I could think was, If only my husband were here, standing beside me. Loneliness would be instantly transformed into romance, emptiness into completeness.

Of course, the big irony was that if Adam *were* here, *I* wouldn't be. I'd still be in sleepy little Santa Paula, where I'd known a different kind of loneliness when I left my L.A. friends of many years to be with a man who was retired, soon ill, and basically a recluse. Being a social person, I found that hard. Our neighbors were all either elderly or Hispanic (the latter with severely limited English). I saw my old pals less and less because it was often hard to leave Adam, and nobody really wanted to drive a hundred miles to my place for dinner.

As I settled into my new life back in L.A., I gradually began to understand that old cliché about life being a series of compromises. I concluded, at the risk of sounding like Norman Vincent Peale, that since we can never have *everything*, why not make the most of what we do have? So I did what Harry Truman would have done: gave myself a good kick in the pants and tried to keep remembering that I'd most assuredly not been forgotten by God.

But it was still a little tough, meeting my L.A. neighbors. While I'm definitely a people person, I also have a streak of shyness that makes it hard for me just to go up to somebody and introduce myself. I'm not like Harry Truman, a gregarious soul who practically invented the handshake. He lived his whole life according to the cornball theory that a stranger was just a friend you hadn't yet met.

Fortunately, in this regard, Truman the dog was a chip off the old block. It was his unshakable belief that every human had been put on the earth solely to meet him. Unlike most other chihuahuas, who tend to greet strangers with snarls and snips—they're notorious as a breed for being owner-exclusive in their affections—Truman's little heart was so big that the whole universe could fit into it. Like Harry Truman, he was completely free of prejudice. He would race up to anyone and everyone, regardless of size, shape, race, color, or creed, willing—indeed, anxious—to talk to them (in his language, anyway).

On his first walk on our new street, he managed to introduce me to my next-door neighbors simply by running right through their open front door. Let me warn you: if you really want to feel like a total fool, buy one of those retractable leashes that supposedly make it possible to reel your dog in like a fish when he's going in a direction you don't want him to. But don't *you* be reeled in; this is pure fantasy. Truman's leash never exhibited any such mythic powers. In fact, it did just the opposite, dragging me kicking and screaming along behind him as he joyfully raced toward the forbidden destination.

So . . . into a total stranger's house we flew.

"Oh, my God, I am so sorry," I exclaimed, as Truman raced over to the bewildered young man on the couch and jumped onto his stomach.

Talk about an icebreaker. "Hey, there!" My neighbor erupted in a deep, wonderful laugh that summoned his wife.

"I'm Mary Beth Crain, your new neighbor," I said, hurriedly introducing myself. "And this is Truman."

"Hey, Truman!" The man tickled Truman's stomach and held out his hand. "I'm Kenny. And this is Susan."

"I'm so glad you stopped by," said Susan, as though it was the most natural thing in the world to have somebody (and somebody's dog) plop as if from the sky into the living room. "I saw your moving truck the other day and was just going to come over and invite you in for iced tea."

Miraculously, Kenny and Susan were the type of people you instantly felt you'd known for about five hundred years. I ended up staying for two hours, and we've been dropping in and out of each other's houses ever since.

We discovered that we had a lot in common. The most

important thing was that all three of us shared the same deranged sense of humor, which meant that they could really appreciate the fact that I was writing this odd little book about a chihuahua that I'd named after Harry Truman. In fact, they were so humored by the project that it wasn't long before the whole neighborhood knew me before I knew them.

"You must be the writer," said Carl, who lived four houses up the road, when I said hello on one of Truman's walks.

"How do you know?" I asked.

"Oh, I heard all about your chihuahua, Truman. You're doing a book on him and Harry Truman, right?"

"You must be the writer," said Phil across the street, as I passed his house with Truman in tow (or was it the other way around?). "And this must be Truman."

Hey, this wasn't bad. I no longer had to worry about introducing myself to anybody; overnight, my dog had made me the celebrity of the block.

Things got even more charming some months later when, after dinner one night at Kenny and Susan's, I read them the chapters in which I'd included them. They laughed so hard that Susan literally fell off the couch and Kenny had to periodically come up for air. They immediately offered their house for a book-signing, and the very next day, when I took Truman on his walk, everybody on the street seemed to have heard about the chapters and wanted to know if they, too, were going to be in the book.

"I hear it's a scream," said Martha, who lived next door to me on the other side. "Kenny and Susan told me they're having a book-signing. When is it?"

Since the book hadn't even been sold yet, I tried to act vague without bursting Martha's bubble.

"We're all going to be famous," she concluded enthusiastically. "Pine Crest Drive! Imagine."

It got to be like those good old days when people would line the docks of New York waiting for the next shipment of magazines carrying the newest installment of a chapter in Charles Dickens's latest opus.

"When can we hear some more chapters?" Kenny wanted to know, watering his lawn.

"Do I get to read it?" asked Phil.

Even Mary down the street, who was about eighty-five, was in on the excitement.

"Actually, I never paid too much attention to Harry Truman," she admitted. "I was too busy raising my kids. And besides, we were from Chicago."

What *that* had to do with anything I couldn't fathom.

"Well, he was a Missourian, you know."

Okay . . .

"But I love dogs. We had the cutest little dog once. I can't wait to read about yours."

Along about this time, the cats decided that they, too, wanted to be part of the act. And so, one evening, without any warning whatsoever, they suddenly appeared and began walking with Truman and me.

"What are you guys doing here?" I asked.

They merely looked up at me, blinked, and continued to march behind Truman.

It was one of those lovely, balmy summer nights when everybody was outside, watering and chatting. As our little procession made its way down the street, all the neighbors cracked up.

A Widow, a Chihuahua, and Harry Truman

"Here comes the family outing!" boomed Carl.

I myself was mystified. Oh, occasionally I'd seen a cat on a walk with a dog. But *my* cats? Who had made it a studied practice not to give Truman the time of day?

Inexplicably, the ritual continues to this day. Petie, Rhonda, Truman, and I—the Pine Crest Parade. Fortunately, now that Truman has been with us for three years, the cats have become much more tolerant of their bratty little brother, condescending, now and then, to lick his nose and even race him down the street. One night I even thought I heard Harry Truman, chuckling delightedly as we took the air. I know just what he would have said, too, if he'd been alive: "If those cats and that dog can walk along arm in arm—well, by God, there's hope for the Democrats and Republicans!"

Chapter 11

The Obedience School Fiasco

My definition of a leader . . . is someone who
can persuade people to do what they don't want to
do, or do what they're too lazy to do and like it.

Quite early on in Truman's and my relationship, it became painfully evident that as far as Harry Truman's definition of leadership was concerned, I was a dismal failure. On the other hand, it's probably considerably easier to make a *man* do what he doesn't want to do than it is a *chihuahua*.

I'm sure that all responsible dog owners live in terrible fear of public censure. I personally quake in my boots every time I take Truman visiting. Will he think that the middle of my friend's five-thousand-dollar Chinese rug is a fine place to do his business? Will he go into one of his inexplicable barking seizures, which practically require sedation (on *both* our parts)? I'm here to tell you that as far as dogs are concerned, no act is too heinous to commit, as long as it gets attention. Can I ever

A Widow, a Chihuahua, and Harry Truman

forget the day that shall live in infamy, when Truman climbed onto my brand-new oak dining-room table and lifted his leg in front of a vase of flowers?

It was, in fact, this appalling incident that propelled me to look for an obedience class ASAP. I found it at the local PETCO and signed us up immediately, at the Lifetime Membership price of only ninety-five dollars. This meant that instead of being limited to eight weeks of training, Truman could go free to every class for the next hundred years, should it prove necessary—which I was afraid it might.

When you're a new widow, the silliest things can remind you of your aloneness. I never expected, for instance, that taking Truman to obedience school would precipitate that aching for Adam that I had thought was beginning, after almost a year, to lessen.

But there Truman and I were, surrounded by couples. Oh, there were a few single moms and dads, but the majority of the participants were husbands and wives with the bewildered expression of con-artist victims who'd been taken lock, stock, and barrel. These poor sods fell into two categories: (1) the childless yuppies who had acquired a dog under the gloriously mistaken assumption that it would satisfy their minimal parental yearnings with an equally minimal outlay of time and energy, and (2) the couples who had gotten a dog for their children, only to quickly come to the horrible realization that they'd just signed up for parenthood all over again.

Among this throng of lost souls crowded into the back of PETCO for a final stab at salvation, I felt both ridiculous and lonely. Ridiculous because it was all too apparent that none of us were really dog owners. It was our dogs who owned us, or we wouldn't be sitting there. And lonely because when you come right down to it, it was kind of tough, raising Truman alone. I thought about what a help it would have been to have a husband to fall back on for walks or feedings or discipline or dog-sitting. Then I thought about how much fun Adam and I would have had with Truman—the snotty comments Adam would have made about him to hide his growing fondness for a nasty, yippy little tweeter, the laughter we would have shared at the mad antics of a crazy puppy and two equally crazy owners who were, despite all their protestations to the contrary, falling hopelessly under its spell.

The first class was for only the owners. Surrounded by bags of birdseed and Puppy Chow, we listened carefully as Marta, our instructor, explained to us How Dogs Think.

"The first thing you need to realize is that what *you're* thinking isn't what your *dog* is thinking," said Marta. "And what your dog is thinking is, 'How can I dominate my owner?'"

A murmur of surprised enlightenment rippled though the group.

"Your dog is always going to try to get the upper hand. And you have to show him who's boss. Now there are many subtle ways he'll try to dominate you. For instance, how many of you play tug-of-war with your dog?"

I raised my hand, along with everybody else.

"And how many of you just end the game and walk away when you've had enough, leaving the dog with the toy?"

We all raised our hands again.

"Uh-huh," Marta affirmed, nodding triumphantly. "Well, did you know that when you let the dog 'win' a game, you've let him think he's top dog? You should *never* let your dog win at tug-of-war, or anything else."

I shuddered as I thought of the countless times Truman and

I had played tug-of-war with my underwear and I'd given in to him out of sheer boredom. How did I know that when he ran around with my panties in his mouth, they had suddenly become a victory flag?

"And how many of you have the problem of your dog pushing you out of the way when you open the door, and rushing ahead of you?"

Since at six whole pounds Truman couldn't very well push anyone out of the way, this, fortunately, wasn't one of *our* problems.

"Well, that's another way your dog is telling you he's boss. In a pack, the alpha dog will always go first and the others will follow. So when your dog is shoving you out of the way, he's daring you to prove your alpha dogship. Remember that if you want to have a happy relationship with your dog, you have to become the alpha dog."

Next we had to go around the room, giving our names and confessing our dog's most outstanding behavioral atrocity.

I was so ashamed that Truman was a year old and not yet toilet-trained, which would have made him the equivalent of about fifteen in human years, that I seriously thought of claiming I'd found him on the street the week before. Thank God, however, I wasn't the only one with housebreaking problems. A woman named Susan was brave enough to admit that her puppy persisted in pooping in one spot on the carpet. She'd tried everything, all in vain. "I even put her dish on the spot," she sighed. "And she'll poop right next to her food!"

A man chimed in that his Akita chow, who was left outside all day, would wait patiently to "go to the restroom" inside when the owners came home. "She's just basically a mess," he blurted.

Other exasperating acts of defiance included barking, digging, hyperactivity, and—of course—not listening to commands. Marta nodded sympathetically and seemed to have lots of answers; by the end of the class she was God.

We were told that subsequent classes would be held in the parking lot of the nearby Coast Federal Bank and that we were to wear something with pockets, to hold treats. We were also told not to get discouraged, that learning commands takes lots of time. "Using their minds is harder work for dogs than playing ball," she reminded us. Hey, it's harder for me too, I thought. She gave us some "homework": simple commands like "Sit" and "Stay" to try on our dogs. And then class was dismissed.

I soon discovered that *command* is a word that must be fully understood and appreciated in order for it to function in the manner it was intended. A command must put the fear of God into your dog, as well as the hope of eternal salvation. It can't be a respectful supplication—or worse, a plea. This is one instance where remembering your manners or doing unto others as you would have them do unto you will get you nowhere fast. The nicer you are, the more ridiculous you'll become in your dog's eyes. For as we know, your dog has one goal and one goal only: to achieve dominance over you. And if you don't adjust the scales in your favor at a tender age, your dog will simply consider you its slave forever.

Of course, his or her contempt will be of an inward nature. On the surface, he'll be all smiles, kisses, and frantic tail wags. But this is a mere facade, one familiar to all repressed peoples who have learned to hide their simmering rage and deadly wit under a veneer of obedient graciousness. Inside, your dog will always be thinking, "Isn't my owner the most pathetic excuse for a living creature you ever saw? I must humor him/her. It's the only decent thing to do."

As I worked through my homework that week, it was clear that Truman didn't have much respect for my commands. In fact, when I tried to make him obey them, he looked at me in utter amazement, as though I'd suddenly begun speaking in tongues. I had to admit that obedience training was simply a tool, not a miracle cure for nine months of unrelieved spoiling. It was useless to try to convince Truman of the virtues of obedience, because he'd done very well up to now going his own merry way. So, yes, mea culpa. I had a willful little potentate on my hands, and the buck stopped here. I could just hear the hallowed voice of the late Barbara Woodhouse, reprimanding me from dog-training heaven. "There are NO BAD DOGS! Only STUPID OWNERS!"

On class night the next week, I got Truman into his little blue harness and off we went. Like any proud mother, I was convinced that he was going to be the most adorable dog there. And I was right. By the time we arrived in the parking lot, most of the class was already in place; and with the exception of two miniature pinschers, who were a few pounds larger than Truman but not nearly as cute, the thirty-odd dogs were all huge beasts. We were greeted with the sounds of frantic barking and equally frantic commands that were, essentially, blowing in the wind. Everybody was engaged in trying to make his or her dog sit, with mixed results. The good dogs—those who had obviously been taught ahead of the game (like the kids in nursery school who were computer-literate by the time they were two)—sat promptly and quietly at their owners' feet. The problem dogs simply stared up at their owners with happy, stupid expressions, or barked wildly and ran around sniffing all the delectable scents that come with a parking lot full of hysterical canines.

Being the tiniest member of the class, Truman was, to put it mildly, terrified. He huddled in my arms until Marta walked over to us.

"No holding the dogs," she reprimanded me gently. "Just put him down and don't encourage him to stay with you. If he tries to jump up on you, move away. Remember, this is obedience training. You can't have an obedient dog if he's in your arms and not on the ground."

With a pain in my heart I put him down. He sniffed around and trembled as a great big dog began barking at him and straining at his leash. Then he lifted his leg and pissed on my shoe.

Yup, I guess you could say we'd definitely gotten off on the wrong foot. Needless to say, the class was a total farce. Truman was too traumatized to do anything except cower behind my legs. I tried and tried to get him to sit, but he wasn't the least bit interested in my commands (or even the promise of a treat). Instead, he looked up at me with big, sad eyes and cried. That did it. Tough love be damned. I picked him up and cuddled him, and chalked the evening up to a nice try.

We never did go back to class. I bought some books and tried home-schooling, which to date hasn't been a resounding success, mainly because Truman just doesn't give a damn. Besides, there's the problem of the cats, who enjoy watching our "lessons" from the kitchen counter and smirking down at poor Truman, as if to say, "All *we* have to do to get *our* treats is look bored." With them as the prevailing role models, I'm effectively doomed.

A Widow, a Chihuahua, and Harry Truman

I'm still not sure which one of us is the alpha dog. Truman does roll over on his back in full submission whenever he sees me, which is a good sign. On the other hand, I often catch him looking at me with a strange expression that could be termed either curious or pitying. But then, there I go, anthropomorphizing again. There may be nothing in that look other than what I read into it. Nothing at all.

Chapter 12

The Monkey's Paw

The only kind of miracles I know about are the ones we work ourselves—with a little help from the Almighty.

There's a famous short story by W. W. Jacobs called "The Monkey's Paw." An old English couple is visited by a friend of the husband's, a colonel who served many years in India. Before he leaves, he gives them an ancient Oriental talisman, a monkey's paw that supposedly grants the bearer three wishes. Scoffing at such superstition, the couple's only son takes the paw and laughingly wishes for two hundred pounds. The paw flies out of his hand and disappears.

The following day a somber man clad in black arrives at the door with the terrible news that the son is dead—mangled in a tractor accident. The life-insurance payment they receive is two hundred pounds.

The old woman goes crazy. She tells her husband to find the monkey's paw so that she can wish their son back from the grave. He's horrified and refuses to look for the loathsome

A Widow, a Chihuahua, and Harry Truman

object, but she finds it and makes her wish. The paw flies into the air again. They hear footsteps coming up the path, growing closer and closer. Then they hear ominous knocking. The husband, knowing that it's their son returning as a mangled ghoul, finds the paw just as his wife is rushing to open the door, and he desperately wishes his son back into the grave. His wife opens the door to . . . nothing but the night wind.

After someone you love dies, you're apt to find yourself trying to make sense of something that doesn't make sense by substituting magical for logical thinking. For instance, I went through a strange, unsettling period when I missed Adam so desperately that I tried to wish him back from the dead.

I guess this is what the grief books refer to as the "bargaining" stage. It fits in the grief process somewhere between denial and depression, when the realization of death has finally sunk in but acceptance of it is still impossible. So you engage in a little haggling with God. You wheedle, you whine, you plead. You say, Lord, you can do anything, right? I mean, you made the whole world in less time than it takes me to clean my house. So what's the big deal about sending one measly little human back to earth? You engineered the Resurrection—now, don't get me wrong, I'm not saying my husband was Jesus or anything. But this doesn't have to be *that* kind of a production. We don't need empty tombs or the heavens opening up and the angels coming down. Just a little miracle, like waking up in the morning and finding him there beside me again.

Having the vivid imagination of a writer, to whom the line between fiction and reality is often as indistinguishable as the lanes on a highway in a blizzard, I'm afraid I might have gone a bit further than the average person in my fantasies. Both Adam and I were *Twilight Zone* freaks, as I've mentioned, and after he died I began to wonder why things that happened in the Zone couldn't happen to me. Old people were always becoming young again; the dead were always coming back to life. Why couldn't the timeline of human existence be so marvelously fluid and malleable? Why, if I tried hard enough, couldn't I, too, wish and wish a miracle into reality?

"Would you really want him back?" my therapist asked gently. "As sick as he was?"

"Not *sick*, Marion. I'd want him back young and healthy." As long as we're talking miracles, why not go for broke?

"But you never knew him when he was young and healthy," she reminded me. "You married a man who was twenty-three years older than yourself, who was a smoker with emphysema, who almost died of double pneumonia six months after you met him. The doctors told you at that time that lung cancer was a definite possibility, didn't they?"

I nodded. "But *not* getting lung cancer, if he quit smoking, was also a possibility. And he did quit."

"You played the odds," Marion said. "And you lost. But you won too. You didn't have the years together that you wanted. But you did have a wonderful marriage. Tell me something: if you had it all to do over—if you knew that Adam was going to die before your third anniversary—would you still have married him?"

"Yes. Oh, yes."

"So it was all worth it?"

"Yes." I paused. "And no."

"How no?"

"I'm not sure that loving someone that much is worth it, when the pain of losing him is so great."

A Widow, a Chihuahua, and Harry Truman

"So it isn't better to have loved and lost than never to have loved at all?"

"I don't know," I conceded, sighing. "I really don't know."

"You will," she said with a smile. "In time you will."

Time. There it was again.

"But he's been dead six months and it doesn't feel any better."

"Six months isn't a very long time," she pointed out. "You know, other cultures allot five *years* for the grieving process to be complete."

"Five years?" I exclaimed. "I couldn't go on feeling this way for five years."

"That's just the point. You don't. It takes five years to *heal*. The healing process is gradual, and it's mysterious. It involves trust—in life and in yourself."

"I feel as if I can't trust *anything* anymore."

"Why?"

"Because. I've been betrayed."

"By whom?"

"By everyone and everything. Life. Love. God. I mean, why bother to trust, or love, if it can all be snatched away in the twinkling of an eye?"

"I don't know." Marion gave me one of her "you've got the answer inside of you" looks. "By the way, how's that puppy of yours doing?"

"Oh, great. You know why?"

"Why?"

"Because he's not asking big, unanswerable questions like this. He doesn't expect anything other than what he gets. So he's never disappointed in life."

"I see," Marion mused. "Has it ever occurred to you that that little chihuahua could be a guru in disguise?"

In spite of myself I began to smile. I didn't want to; I was angry and sad and determined to stay that way if being happy meant I'd be accepting Adam's awful death and maybe even beginning to forget him. But even in my humorless state, I had to acknowledge the Zen absurdity of the situation.

"Yeah," I snorted. "Swami Mahatma Truman. I should put him on the circuit. He could sit on a little velvet cushion and chew on his tinkly bone, and hundreds of thousands would achieve enlightenment."

"One is enough," Marion said gently. "You know, I believe that animals always come into our lives to teach us something we need to learn at that particular moment. And that," she looked at her watch, "is all I'm going to say about it."

A Widow, a Chihuahua, and Harry Truman

Chapter 13

How Dumb Is Your Dog?

I'm not one to insist that a man can't possibly
make it without a lot of formal education, since my
own formal education pretty much stopped when
I graduated from Independence High School.

Perhaps one of the things Truman had to teach me was
the difference between what we can control and what we can't.

If you think that because we humans are born with the ca-
pacity for reason, we automatically exercise that faculty, surprise. When it comes to trying to fit life into the neat little
package of what we think it should be, reason can scream at us
until it's blue in the face, only to be politely and calmly silenced
by the irrational mind.

Even though reason told me I couldn't have controlled
Adam's lifespan or prevented his death, I still tormented myself by looking for ways I could have played God. Even though
reason told me I couldn't work miracles like bringing Adam

back to life, I still went to bed at night hoping to see his dear face in the morning.

And even though reason told me that Truman's brain power, or lack thereof, was no reflection on me, I found myself feeling acute embarrassment when he seemed to be, shall we say, slow for his age.

Yes, at times it's occurred to me, not without considerable pain, that Truman might not be the brightest dog in the world. This is surprisingly hard for a dog owner to admit. You'd think we wouldn't care; after all, we don't have to plan for a future at Yale, or worry about whether he'll get a good job someday. But you'd be amazed at how personally one can take one's dog's failings.

Truman's challenged intellectual state became obvious in various subtle ways. First of all, he seemed to have no English comprehension whatsoever. I'd met other dogs who knew the names of their toys, for example, and would run to get whatever you told them to. And what dog doesn't respond to "Want to take a WALK?" as if it were the music of the spheres?

But Truman just didn't get it. When I'd say, "Want to take a walk?" he'd look at me as blankly as though I'd asked him to comment on Plato's discourses. And long were the hours I spent trying to get him to bring his toys over. "Truman, go get Doggie Dog!" I'd say, picking up his little stuffed puppy and holding it in the air. "Look, Truman. This is Doggie Dog! And this"—I'd grab his squeaky mouse—"is Mousy Mouse! And this"—out came the rubber duck—"is Ducky Duck!"

Truman would cock his head. You could almost hear the wheels creaking as he struggled heroically to understand.

"Now," I'd say, putting them all on the floor. "Go get Doggie Dog!"

A Widow, a Chihuahua, and Harry Truman

Truman would just stand there, tail wagging, head still cocked. Was he ruminating? Lazy? Or just plain dumb? Unfortunately, it was I who felt like the idiot as I went through the routine again and again while Truman stood there watching with a big dog grin, obviously enjoying my performance.

Then there was the issue of fetching. When I got Truman, I eagerly looked forward to the day we'd be able to engage in sporting activities together. I had misty visions of us in the park, playing catch or Frisbee with other happy dogs and owners. But when, after a year, he still had no idea what "Fetch!" meant, I was deeply concerned. I'd sit there for half an hour, throwing wads of Kleenex in the air and yelling, "Go get it, Truman!" Eyes glowing with excitement, muscles quivering, Truman would fixate on the trophy until it left my hand. Then he'd go flying after it. But the game ended there. He'd grab the Kleenex, shake it vigorously, and drop it, running back to me as if to say, "Throw another one!"

"Bring it back here, Truman," I'd command. *Command.* Hah! "Come on, honey. Bring it here. I can't throw it again unless you bring it to me."

Again, the disturbingly blank look. I felt somewhat like a missionary among the savages of Borneo, trying to explain to them the benefit of putting on clothes and acting sensible.

Did it occur to me that Truman was actually not stupid at all, but was in fact getting me to do his bidding, saving himself an extra trip at my expense? Yes, it did. (I must admit that I'm *still* not sure what the truth is.) My only solace was that a whole lot of people thought Harry Truman wasn't too bright either. Little did they know that by the age of fourteen, Harry had read all thirty-five hundred books in the Independence Public Library. And, having a photographic memory, he could quote whole passages from them sixty years later. This gave me hope regarding his namesake. It was entirely possible that Truman, too, was an unrecognized genius, behind whose naive exterior gigantic plots of mastermind quality were being secretly engineered. On the other hand . . . But I preferred not to think about that.

Then there was the dismal day that a new friend of mine, Joanna, came over with her chihuahua, Buddy Boy. Joanna arrived bearing gifts of flowers and Pupperoni, a treat that looks, smells, and presumably tastes like what the name suggests, the promise of which encourages dogs to outdo themselves in all pursuits.

Buddy Boy was obviously a Pupperoni pro. "Watch this," Joanna said, holding a tempting morsel high in the air. "Buddy! Dance."

Buddy Boy spun round and round in graceful if frantic pirouettes, a veritable Arthur Murray of the dog world.

"Roll over!" Joanna commanded. Buddy Boy promptly fell on the floor and rolled over, not once but twice.

"Good boy!" Joanna beamed. "Now . . . jump!"

Buddy Boy skyrocketed upward and caught the Pupperoni in midair.

Reason told me that Buddy Boy was Buddy Boy and Truman was Truman. But envy seized my heart.

"Does Truman do tricks?" asked Joanna.

"Uh, no. I mean, I've never tried to teach him any," I mumbled.

"Buddy is so bright. He learns tricks in only a few minutes."

"That's great." I could just imagine trying to teach Truman such advanced maneuvers. There we'd be, twenty years from now, both of us old and gray, me still holding a piece of Pupperoni in the air with shaking hands, croaking, "Dance, Truman!" as he sat there, eyes dim with age but still blank as ever.

"What can Truman do?" Joanna wanted to know.

"Uh, well, he sits. Sometimes."

"Oh. Truman! Here, Truman!" Joanna held up a piece of Pupperoni. Truman looked up excitedly.

"Sit, Truman!"

Truman stood there, bestowing his vaguest look upon Joanna. I felt like killing him.

"Sit, Truman!" Joanna repeated, as Buddy Boy looked on smugly. Truman continued to stand at full attention, eyes on the prize.

"Have you tried obedience school?" Joanna asked kindly. "Of course, Buddy didn't need it. He learns so quickly. But I hear it's really helpful."

"We tried it," I muttered. "There were too many big dogs there and he, uh, couldn't concentrate."

"Well, maybe you could find another class."

Yeah, I thought. For Dog Retards. Or maybe Owner Retards.

"Come on, Buddy!" Joanna turned to her little Einstein. "Sit!"

In a final slap to Truman's and my already battered pride, Buddy Boy plopped his butt smack down on the floor.

"Truman's still young," I fumbled, in a last-ditch attempt at face-saving. "He's not quite a year."

"Buddy's just a little over a year," Joanna said. "And he learned tricks at six months."

Oh, well. After the genius and his mother had left, I took out a piece of Pupperoni.

"Okay, Truman. Sit!" I held the Pupperoni to his nose and pushed his butt down. "Good dog." I gave him the treat and took out another. Truman jumped up.

"No. Sit!"

He ignored me and made for the Pupperoni.

"No! *Sit!*" I pushed his butt down. He promptly raised it. This ridiculous game of seesaw continued until Truman barked at me, rudely, loudly, and emphatically, as if to say, "Sit, my ass. Drop it!"

That was the last straw. "You little shit!" I yelled. "You act like an idiot and humiliate me and now you have the nerve to *bark* at me?"

I glared down at him. He glared up at me, rear end raised high in a gesture of supreme defiance.

"You're not getting any Pupperoni until you SIT!" I growled.

Resentment blazed from Truman's eyes. He barked again. I stood my ground, though; and then, right before my disbelieving eyes, he sat.

I wanted to dance around like Buddy Boy. Instead, however, I maintained my composure and merely praised him with a "Good dog!" and handed him the treat. He gobbled it up and continued to sit, in obedient anticipation of the next installment.

"No, Truman. That's all. All gone."

He began to whine. Then he jumped up and ran off, without waiting, of course, to be released from the sit command. *That* happy day would undoubtedly not come in *my* lifetime, I reflected.

It's now over two years later, and I'm proud to report that Truman is still sitting for his Pupperoni—*only,* however, for his Pupperoni. But I've come to the conclusion that this isn't a matter of stupidity. On the contrary, Truman simply doesn't see the payoff in sitting just for the sake of sitting or, God forbid, just because it would please me. He's a show-me-the-money type of dog, which, if anything, is indicative of advanced reasoning. So I feel *much* better.

Chapter 14

Truman Escapes

It requires eternal watchfulness to preserve liberty.

One of the most daunting challenges puppyhood presents is a naughty dog that won't come when you call him.

The obvious cure for this maddening behavior is, of course, obedience school. But we all know how Truman fared with that. I felt like the mother of a preschool dropout. The only alternative to the classroom was the streets, a dangerous place indeed for a two-year-old.

But the streets were where Truman most wanted to be. The wide world beckoned every moment; liberty's call was loud and insistent, from the moment his sloppy kisses woke me up until the moment I hit the pillow at night, worn out from another day of trying to keep my little bundle of joy from shooting out a door inadvertently left open for two seconds or leaping out a window that didn't properly latch.

Yes, in the realm of escape artists, Truman deserved the Houdini Award. It came, no doubt, from observing the cats. I used to feel sorry for little Truman as he watched, eyes filled with longing, while his feline siblings bounded airily onto the cabinet under the dining-room window, and then onto the sill, where they'd push the window open with a well-timed flick of the paw and disappear into the tantalizing great outdoors.

I had no idea that Truman was capable of following the cats' carefully mapped out route to freedom. His hopes of imitating their high jumps were always about as realistic as my winning the pole-vaulting medal at the Olympics. But when I looked outside one bright spring morning, what did I see but Mr. Truman frolicking gaily about in the garden!

I ran out and grabbed him. He looked absolutely crestfallen at his premature capture, and it was an exercise in futility, I knew, to try to explain to him why the cats could be trusted outside and he couldn't. I brought him in, closing the door carefully behind us, and looked around to discover his means of escape. I saw the open window and dismissed it. There was no way he could have made his way up onto the cabinet underneath, unless he had suddenly become a cat or a member of the Peking Opera.

But a little while later the mystery was solved, when I happened to see Truman jump up onto a chair near the window. From this vantage point it was a straight shot onto the cabinet and the windowsill, where he started pushing the faulty latch open with his nose.

"Damn those cats," I muttered, whisking Truman up and giving him a good scolding. After that I had the latch fixed and made a careful tour of the house, puppy-proofing it against any more possible breakouts. My paranoia got so bad that I took to turning off the TV when movies like *The Great Escape* or *Breakout* were on. Truman didn't need any more ideas.

But as Greek tragedy could have told me, destiny is stronger than human ingenuity. Or, as my wise Jewish grandmother loved to observe, "Man proposes; God disposes." It was inevitable that one day Truman would accomplish his most cherished mission. And in this case, the deus ex machina took the form of the cable guy.

"Hey, Killer!" he greeted Truman as he walked in. He probably thought he was being original, but for some mysterious reason every handyman who'd ever come over, from the plumber to the painters, called my dog Killer.

I grabbed Truman, who was about to dart out the open door. "We have to make sure the door's closed," I explained. "He loves to make a run for it."

"Sure," the cable guy agreed, guffawing. "We wouldn't want Killer here gettin' loose and terrorizing the neighborhood, would we?"

It was obvious that he didn't appreciate the seriousness of the situation. And neither did his co-workers, a couple of garrulous dudes in bandannas who, within mere minutes, left the door wide open when they went out to go up on the roof.

His long-awaited exit at hand, Truman was out the door in a flash.

"Oh, my God!" I screamed, racing out after him. "Truman! Come back here!"

But Truman flew down the driveway and into the street, merrily ignoring my frantic calls.

"Hey! Killer!" The cable guy joined me in the chase, followed by his remorseful buddies. By this time one of the neighbors, a grand older lady named May, had come out on her porch to see what all the commotion was about.

"Truman!" she hollered. "You bad boy! Get back here!"

A Widow, a Chihuahua, and Harry Truman

As we raced down the street, a girl who was sitting on her porch offered to help.

"I've got a leash," she said, "and some dog biscuits." So she joined the posse, which was rapidly assuming the appearance of a Keystone Cops farce—a motley cast of characters huffing and puffing behind a little chihuahua with huge ears flying in the breeze and a triumphant grin on his face.

It was no use. The more we all pleaded and cajoled, the faster he ran. Pooped, I finally had to stop. The cable guys raised the white flag too, apologizing and saying they had to get back to work. The girl from the porch patted me on the shoulder.

"Don't worry," she said. "He'll come back."

I watched helplessly as Truman neared the dangerous main thoroughfare of Monterey Road. My dog had run away and was going to get killed, and there was nothing I could do about it.

After Adam and Angel, the thought of losing Truman was too much for me. Until that moment I hadn't quite realized just how deeply into my heart he had burrowed. Suddenly I couldn't imagine life without his morning kisses, his treasure pile, his menagerie of stuffed toys, his bottomless love that had so often supplied me with that extra ounce of strength I needed to keep on going.

I stood there defeated, tears streaming down my cheeks. Then I saw something way in the distance, something that seemed like a mirage. But it was *real*. Truman had turned around and was racing toward me!

"Sweetheart!" I cried, as he bounded into my arms. Although he deserved a good old-fashioned licking, I was the one who got one—all over my face and glasses. We stood there like a couple of auld eejits, covering each other with kisses. The girl from the porch gave me the thumbs-up.

"See?" she said triumphantly. "I told you!"

When we got back to my house, May came over to us and shook her finger at the delinquent. "Well, Truman," she boomed. "You're not running for president. You're running for Monterey Road!"

May's dog, an ancient, crabby terrier named Geraldine, watched us grumpily from behind her own screen door.

"Truman, why the hell can't you be good like Geraldine?" I sighed. "*She'd* never run off like that."

"Oh, he's still just a puppy," May said. "Geraldine was the same way once. But she outgrew it, and he will too. You just wait. There'll come a day when he grows up and does everything you want him to."

"Yeah, I think it's called the Second Coming," I said.

But there did indeed come a day when Truman grew up, a day when he was quiet, mature, and obedient, a day when he no longer dragged his stuffed cat from room to room or chewed the TV wires or raced around the house in whirling-dervish circles, letting off puppy steam. It was a bittersweet day, colored by both relief and mourning. I could look back on puppyhood and say I'd survived it. But at the same time I missed its madcap surprises, its wild, uninhibited energy, its standing invitation to abandon my maturity and feel, once more, what it was like to be uncorrupted by experience and in love with each waking moment.

Truman and I escorted May home, and Truman sniffed at Geraldine through the screen door. She growled.

"Geraldine! You stop it!" May scolded her. "That's what happens when you get old," she said. "The least little thing gets on your nerves."

"I'm getting that way myself," I said.

A Widow, a Chihuahua, and Harry Truman

"You?" May snorted. "You're just a kid."

As we said goodbye, she called after me, "Enjoy it while it lasts."

"What?"

"You know. Being young."

I wanted to tell May that I was forty-six and felt every bit of it. Often I felt weary. Sometimes my joints ached and I walked slowly. After the Angel of Death had visited my house, life suddenly seemed so fragile that I began to see my existence in terms of days, weeks, or months instead of years. I began reading the obituaries, something my grandmother used to do, and calculating average ages of death. Women younger than I were dying like flies, of breast cancer, heart attacks, you name it. Who was I to assume that I was any less vulnerable to destruction?

But then there was May, some seventy-odd years old and tough as shoe leather, still duking it out despite crippling rheumatoid arthritis and a variety of other unpleasantnesses. And I was to her what Truman was to Geraldine—a young pup. Maybe things weren't so bad after all. Maybe I *did* still have a life before me.

Then I took Truman inside and promptly collapsed on the couch. It had been one hell of an afternoon, and I felt about ninety years old. I could enjoy being young tomorrow, I decided. Right now I needed a nap.

Chapter 15

Truman Goes Hollywood

If a man has the right woman for a partner,
he never has any trouble.

One of the most important things Truman gave me was
the sense of feeling needed again.

I had been Adam's life, and he had been mine. When he
died, I was suddenly left without someone to care for. This is a
hard reality that widows often have to face. To whom, now, do
you give all that love that's still burning inside of you?

Grief hadn't pushed me so far over the edge that my dog
actually became a substitute husband or a surrogate child. But
I never ceased to be amazed at how attached he was to me and
me alone. Even though it was sometimes annoying, even exasperating, it was also enormously comforting to know that I
was once again the most important thing in someone's life. If
you've owned only cats, you can't imagine the bond a dog
forges with a human, a bond that both enslaves and ennobles.
I've always been the independent type, in whom the words
schedule and *routine* immediately inspire terror, which was

why I'd never felt inclined toward either dog ownership or parenthood. But my days of being a footloose and fancy-free cat owner came to an abrupt end the moment Truman entered my life.

He had to be everywhere I was—sitting against me, on top of me, or in my arms. "He's like an attachment," one of my friends observed. It was as if I'd grown a third arm or leg. My pet-sitter Pat's ominous warning—"You'll be wearing that dog!"—came back to haunt me. If I tried to work at the computer, Truman would jump up and down as if on a pogo stick, trying to get into my lap. When that didn't work, he'd paw at my legs and whimper until I gave in and picked him up. I'm ashamed to admit that there were many days I typed with one hand and held Truman with the other. But that was better than the crying and pestering.

The worst thing was how intently he watched me. His eyes were glued to my every move and I felt like I was on constant display. It was, as I somewhat cynically termed it, "out of sight, out of mind": whenever I was out of his sight, he would go out of his mind. The most annoying thing was going to the bathroom. If I closed the door, Truman would stand outside and wail pathetically until I opened it. Then he would stand in the doorway, watching *me* do *my* business. In a way it was tit for tat, I guess, but it was still unnerving.

The degree of his dependency was scary. I found myself feeling guilty if I went out for coffee. It didn't help to read all the articles I encountered about dogs and separation anxiety; every pet magazine, it seemed, had at least one feature or column devoted to readers' horror stories about dogs going crazy and chewing up the furniture, the walls, or themselves when their owners left them for an afternoon.

So you can imagine *my* anxiety when I had to leave Truman for a month to go to Ireland. What was I going to do? I couldn't put him in a kennel for a whole month, and my sitter couldn't take him to her house. Fortunately, fate intervened, finding not only the perfect sitter but the perfect bride for Truman.

I'm firmly convinced that it's only in L.A. that your chihuahua could meet and marry a movie star. The movie star I'm referring to is Poppy Burton, the chihuahua of Tim Burton, the director of *Edward Scissorhands, Batman, The Nightmare Before Christmas, Beetlejuice,* and other offbeat megahits.

Poppy, Tim's pride and joy, was a pretty little cream-colored chihuahua, the kind that's been granted immortality thanks to those Taco Bell commercials. Any of you who saw *Mars Attacks!* will remember her as the yippy little dog of bubble-headed reporter Sarah Jessica Parker. Poppy's crowning moment in the movie came when, in a brilliant coup of Burtonesque weirdness, the Martians abducted the two of them and transplanted Poppy's head onto Sarah Jessica's body, and Sarah Jessica's head onto Poppy's body.

So anyway, how did Truman and Poppy meet? Well, I'd become a friend of a woman named Gurmukh Khalsa, a Sikh who lived in the middle of Hollywood and taught yoga to the stars. Some of her more recognizable clients included Madonna, David Duchovny, Courtney Love, and Tim Burton and his girlfriend, actress Lisa Marie. Gurmukh had introduced another Sikh, a woman by the name of Sant Kaur, to Tim, and this fortuitous meeting had led to Sant Kaur's becoming Tim's personal assistant.

Among Sant Kaur's most important duties was babysitting Poppy, as well as Lisa Marie's chihuahua, Violet, a tiny little creature with unusual gray-spotted markings and even more unusual violet eyes—hence her name. To add to her odd looks, Violet also had a tongue that was too big and always hung out the side of her mouth, giving her a slightly idiotic look. In the realm of nervous chihuahuas, Violet was the queen. Weighing in at only three pounds, she was terrified of everything and spent most of her time buried behind a pillow on the couch, a tiny ear or tail protruding as a warning sign lest someone sit down on the pillow and crush her to death.

Now this is how God works: when I was desperately looking for a sitter for Truman, Gurmukh came to the rescue and suggested Sant Kaur—who, as it turned out, was also sitting for Poppy and Violet while Tim and Lisa Marie were in Europe. So that's how Truman hooked up with Poppy Burton. And what a hooking up it was.

Sant Kaur confided to me that one of Tim's dearest wishes was for Poppy to have a puppy. This, however, had proved to be a formidable challenge. At the age of nearly four, Poppy had never been pregnant, owing largely to the fact that she was so haughty that she wouldn't let any male near her, whether or not she was in heat. Whenever one approached, she'd turn on him with a repertoire of growls, snarls, and teeth-baring that sent the prospective suitor running for the nearest cover.

But by some miracle, Poppy took a shine to Truman. Whether it was his good looks or his winning disposition, I can't say. But when I returned from Ireland, Sant Kaur reported the exciting news that Poppy and Truman were an item, and that Tim Burton was very impressed. In fact, when she suggested that the two of them get together on the occasion of Poppy's next heat, Tim was all for it. "If Truman can hang in there, he's got the job," were his words, as relayed to me.

Needless to say, I was gung ho too. Truman, the husband of a movie star! I immediately went out and rented *Mars Attacks!* It was most thrilling to see Poppy on screen. In fact, by the time the great day arrived, I was so sick of *Mars Attacks!* I can't tell you, as I'd rented it approximately twenty times to show all my friends Truman's bride-to-be.

Several months later, Sant Kaur called to tell me that Poppy was in heat and that Tim had asked if Truman could be pressed into service. You betcha! So that weekend, I arrived at her apartment, stud in tow.

Boy was Poppy glad to see Truman. Within three seconds she was sniffing and licking him and showing off her rear end with absolutely no shame.

As for Truman, well, he knew just what to do. He sniffed the sacred goods and began to lick them, right in front of everyone. Though I knew what we were there for, his behavior shocked me. He was only eleven months old, for God's sake! To me he was still in diapers. And suddenly there he was, the envy of canine Hollywood. I mean, sunrise, sunset, swiftly flow the minutes!

For about an hour, Truman and Poppy went around in circles, noses to behinds. Every once in awhile Truman would attempt to mount Poppy and she would obligingly stand at attention. But that lasted only a couple of seconds, at which point she would turn on him for no apparent reason, snarling and snapping in her best Joan Crawford imitation.

"No wonder the other guys gave up," I said to Sant Kaur. "She's a real prima donna."

Truman, however, was not in the least discouraged. Perhaps it was because he was a much younger man; it was, after all, the equivalent of a mature woman seducing a seven-year-old. While Poppy alternated between beckoning him, chasing him, and turning on him, Truman just kept dancing around her and bouncing back for more. Meanwhile, Violet sat primly on a cushion, surveying the proceedings with great interest, while Missy, Sant Kaur's beautiful border collie, lay there calmly and seemed to smile down on the happy couple with regal beneficence. It was quite a scene. I wondered if Tim Burton might be up for making a movie with the four of them, perhaps a sort of doggie *Four Stooges*.

By three o'clock things were heating up. Truman was panting and drooling and had made progress along the rear flank, managing to get up on his tippytoes and hump his amour. Unfortunately, he kept missing the mark and ending up on her thigh, which made her quite impatient. She would pull away in disgust, like Mae West in the midst of a bad lay. You could almost hear her drawling, "Listen, Big Boy, what good is it when it's way the hell over in Cincinnati?"

And then it happened. Truman grabbed Poppy around the waist and hit the bull's-eye. Poppy let out a yelp, and Sant Kaur and I erupted in cheers. Truman looked over at us as if we were insane and continued to pump away.

"It's 3:07 P.M.!" Sant Kaur clocked the exact moment of the sacred union. "August 24th, 1997, at 3:07 P.M. Wait till Tim hears. He'll be so excited!"

Just about then we realized that the sacred union seemed sealed in cement.

"Uh-oh." Sant Kaur turned to me. "They're stuck. What do we do?"

"Don't look at me," I said.

Poppy yelped and stuck her behind up in the air. Truman was in her up to the hilt; now he turned around, until they were rear to rear, and stuck his behind up too. But being smaller than Poppy, he ended up half off the floor.

After a few minutes Sant Kaur put in a call to pet emergency. The woman who answered assured us that all was going according to God's plan and we shouldn't interfere. Eventually, she said, they would disengage by themselves. So for another half-hour the newlyweds stood back to back like Siamese twins joined at the butt. Fortunately, they didn't seem at all unhappy. On the contrary, Truman was drooling away, his eyes glazed over and a big, happy grin on his face, while Poppy was fairly purring with ecstasy.

"Look at her. She's a changed person already!" said Sant Kaur.

Finally Truman popped out and the two lovers went off by themselves to reflect upon their earth-shattering experience.

"My God. Truman's going to be a father," I said, gazing down at my little boy, who looked back up at me with his usual innocent expression. I thought about his remarkable feat and knew that Harry Truman would have been proud of him. He might even have awarded him the Congressional Medal of Honor, for going where no man had gone before and succeeding where all others had failed.

When I left Sant Kaur's on my own a bit later—Truman was staying on with her not only to finish his work but because I was going to San Francisco in a few days—Poppy was following Truman around and wouldn't let him out of her sight. He was obviously in for quite a honeymoon. I called to him to say goodbye, but for the first time he didn't even notice me. I felt an odd tug at my heart, remembering the old refrain, "A son is a son till he takes a wife . . ." On the other hand, when Poppy suddenly jumped up on my leg, wanting to be taken up, I realized that I hadn't lost a son, I'd gained a daughter.

When I called later in the week to check on Truman, the latest bulletin was that he and Poppy had "done it" at least seven times since the first round. He had slept with his bride faithfully until she returned home and had cried all day after Poppy left. Oh, yes, and Sant Kaur's twelve-year-old daughter, Amrit Sangeet, and her friend had decided that Truman and Poppy needed a proper wedding. They'd married them in a little ceremony, complete with a veil for Poppy, a tie for Truman, and appropriate songs and prayers.

At the moment I called, Amrit Sangeet and her pals were blasting a rap song and teaching Truman to dance to it.

"Oh, my God, his little head is going to the music!" Sant Kaur was clearly enthralled. "He is so cute!"

I hung up, feeling torn. I was vastly relieved that Truman obviously could live very well without me. At the same time, I felt worried and bleak. What if he didn't really need me anymore? How could I compete with Poppy and Missy and all the fun and excitement of life at Sant Kaur's?

But when I went to pick Truman up the next week, he got so hysterical at the sight of me that I thought he was going to explode.

"He missed you," Sant Kaur said, smiling.

"With Poppy and Violet and Amrit Sangeet and her friends fussing over him? He *never* has fun like that at home."

"It doesn't matter. You're his mother. Nobody can take your place." I held Truman tightly and didn't even mind the idea of wearing him for the rest of my life. He loved me. More than anybody. He really did.

Chapter 16

Chihuahua Fashion

The moment my father could afford it he switched from ready-made suits to clothes made up for him by the best tailors. And when he was a senator, he was on the list of the ten best dressed men in the Senate.

—*Margaret Truman*

I'd let my appearance slide after Adam died. The more weight I gained, the more self-esteem I lost, until an ironic thing happened. Although I was bigger than ever, I began to feel invisible, as though I was hardly worth noticing.

And I dressed accordingly. Big T-shirts and baggy pants became my uniform; I couldn't imagine wearing a dress, let alone fitting into one. My recklessness about my appearance was not, however, a result of my weight. I've known many large women who dress smashingly and are utterly alluring. But I was in hiding. Behind the nondescript clothes and the extra pounds lurked the "real" me—the funny, upbeat, "full of bubbles" woman Adam had loved. But she was afraid to come out, afraid of falling in love again and risking another loss she knew she couldn't endure.

It was too bad, because I actually do love clothes. Once upon a time, when I was quite thin and sexy, I'd been a regular fashion plate, reveling in tight jeans and boots, slinky skirts with slits, teeny-weeny bikinis, and other medals of honor bestowed upon the slender of society. But now, even though I could have dressed smartly (even sexily) despite my weight, my heart wasn't in it. So I did the next best thing: I started dressing up Truman instead.

I first discovered the power of chihuahua fashion with Truman's turtleneck sweaters. I had bought two—sky blue and flaming red—ostensibly for functional purposes, since chihuahuas can do annoying things like freeze to death when the temperature goes below seventy. These ridiculous-looking things probably took somebody two minutes and thirty seconds to knit, cost me ten to fifteen bucks, and made Tru-Tru look très fey, fitting around his behind like a skirt. You could almost hear the cats guffawing. No wonder Truman struggled like a two-year-old when I tried to stuff him into a sweater. But I have to say, once the ordeal was over it was worth it. He looked so cute that he could snarl traffic: whenever we were stopped at a light and he was perched upright, paws on the window, people in the cars around us would go crazy, waving, pointing, and laughing, until somebody behind us would honk, angrily reminding us that the light had turned green awhile back.

When he's dressed up, Truman reminds me of Freddy Bartholomew in *Little Lord Fauntleroy*. "Fauntleroy, Mama's Boy!" was a popular taunt at the turn of the century, used to denote a sissy, the kind that wore Fauntleroy suits, those velvet waistcoat and knee-pant horrors with the frilly lace necks that Frances Hodgson Burnett's bestseller made de rigueur attire for a whole generation of unfortunate little boys. Speaking of which, are there such things as Fauntleroy suits for chihuahuas? I must look into it, especially if I move to West Hollywood. Can you imagine Tru-Tru doing Santa Monica Boulevard in a Fauntleroy suit?

Truman's snazziest outfit is definitely his bomber jacket with a knit scarf in blazing red, à la the Red Baron. The jacket, a tiny replica of an Eighth Air Force brown leather jacket, complete with fake lamb's-wool collar and an insignia with the cartoon face of a dopey-looking pooch on the shoulder, is a hand-me-down from Buddy Boy. (You remember, my friend Joanna's genius chihuahua.) At one time Buddy cut quite a figure in it, but unfortunately he'd recently grown so stout that Joanna couldn't fasten the Velcro straps around his expanded little middle; so she graciously donated it to Truman. The scarf came from my next-door neighbor Susan, an ace with the knitting needles, who went berserk when I paraded Truman by in the jacket.

"He's got to have a scarf to go with it," she insisted.

"How about goggles and one of those Flying Leatherneck caps while you're at it?" grunted Kenny.

Unlike me, Susan is one of those amazing women of action. The next morning she knocked on my door, splendid little red scarf in hand. It even had three tassels on either end.

"I knitted it last night," she said. "I just had to. You know."

Yeah, I know. Once you get to dressing up your chihuahua, it's worse than Barbie. Outfits come to you in flashes of inspiration—outfits that you just can't live without. Your dog can, but you can't.

A Widow, a Chihuahua, and Harry Truman

The really embarrassing thing is when you start hanging around the baby-clothes sections of department stores and asking the clerks what would be appropriate for a six-pound boy. You soon learn just how expensive it is to have a new-born—I mean, one that's properly turned out. I was awfully tempted by some tiny blue socks and a set of doll-size overalls. But at twelve bucks a pair for the socks and forty for the overalls, my bargain-basement alter ego rebelled. Which was when I discovered garage sales.

One summer morning Susan and Kenny had a yard sale. I ended up buying a couple of their videos and a tape deck and was just about to leave when my eye fell on a tempting array of baby clothes. These had belonged to Susan's grandson, David, and were going for fifty cents apiece. Now if you were me, could you have resisted the infant sleeper, undershirt, and baby cap, all for only a dollar fifty? I ran next door and grabbed Truman for a fitting. David, who was now two and a half, was absolutely fascinated by the new occupant of his former wardrobe.

"Baby!" he shouted, pointing to Truman, whose nose was peeking out from beneath the white wool cap with a ball on top. And then, confused, he muttered, "Dog!"

The sleeper was a little on the big side too, but that only added to its appeal. As soon as he saw me get it out, Truman would roll over on his back with his legs in the air. I would slip his paws into the arm holes and snap the crotch and off he would toddle, the rear portion hanging down to his feet like an extremely tacky evening gown. This never failed to elicit screams of delight from my friends, and blinks of utter contempt from the cats, who occasionally looked as though they almost felt sorry for Truman and his completely shredded dignity.

The tiny undershirt was a real gem. This had belonged to Susan's little niece, whose grandmother had dyed the family name, Ruiz, on it. The result was what I referred to as Truman's homeboy outfit. All that was missing was the tattoos.

Susan's daughter, Marcie, was delighted, as I'd been her only customer all day.

"I made a dollar fifty," she said. "Who's complaining?"

"Hey, Marcie, I know what was wrong," cackled Kenny. "You put 'Baby Clothes' on the sign. That's why nobody wanted 'em. That sign shoulda read 'Chihuahua Clothes.' They'd a been gone in a second!"

Unfortunately, there was probably more truth in Kenny's statement than sensible people would like to admit. This was when the chihuahua craze was just cranking into full gear following that Taco Bell commercial. Chihuahua articles were plastered on the front pages of newspapers, Target was selling a line of chihuahua T-shirts, and there was apparently such a waiting list at pet stores that the going price for chihuahuas had soared from six hundred to as much as two thousand dollars. When you took your chihuahua for a walk, crowds gathered to gawk admiringly and yell out, "*Yo quiero* Taco Bell!" as if you'd never heard it before.

"If I hear one more '*Yo quiero* Taco Bell,' I'm going to go insane," Joanna, Buddy Boy's mom, confided to me. "Do you get it too?"

"Oh, only about a hundred times a day," I replied. It reminded me of a friend of my late husband, who'd had the unfortunate name of John Doody. He lived his whole life being greeted with, "Howdy, Doody!" And each time people said it, he told us, they acted as if they thought they'd coined the phrase.

A Widow, a Chihuahua, and Harry Truman

Fortunately, I found out that I wasn't the only chihuahua owner who haunted yard sales. One day Joanna invited Truman over to play with Buddy Boy and to see the new addition to his wardrobe.

"Buddy has pants," she announced, holding up a tiny pair of what looked like underwear, with a multicolored fish pattern.

"Where did you get those?" I asked, amazed.

"At a yard sale. They're infant swim trunks!"

Joanna had cut a hole in the rear end for Buddy's tail, and they fit perfectly. Actually, they were functional; Buddy, like Truman, had the exasperating habit of pissing in other people's houses, and Joanna had ingeniously hit upon the solution.

"He won't pee with his trunks on," she said proudly.

A few minutes later Truman lifted his leg in the corner.

"Truman!" I yelled. Rats. Too late.

"It's okay," said Joanna. "I'll put pants on him too. I bought two pairs."

Poor Truman. He struggled vainly as Joanna put him into a pair of baby trunks with a floral pattern. I don't need to tell you that it was quite a sight, Buddy and Truman toddling around with their rear ends ablaze in brightly colored fish and flowers. I thanked God the cats weren't around; they probably would have died of a laughing fit.

I asked Joanna if she ever felt silly, buying clothes for Buddy.

"Are you kidding?" she said. "My philosophy is, anything that small has to be dressed up."

I totally agree. Of course, when we start having chihuahua fashion shows, complete with runways, you can put us away. But until then, I'd say we're just normal moms.

Chapter 17

Truman Comes Out

Three things lead to the ruination of a man:
power, money and women.

I guess I should consider myself lucky, because according to Harry Truman's theory of ruination, Truman was in the clear. He didn't give a hoot about power or money, and when it came to women—well, let's just say that they weren't his top priority.

After the episode with Poppy, I naturally assumed that Truman liked girls, period. This just goes to show how much I know about dogs. Probably a select number of weirdos who are reading this book saw the famous *South Park* episode in which Stan's dog turns gay and poor Stan becomes the local laughingstock. Well, I'm here to tell you that this stuff really happens. The dog you thought was a model little hetero can suddenly turn into a perfectly happy homosexual with nary a backward glance. I should know. It happened to me.

The unlikely object of Truman's adoration was Buster, a tiny, four-pound chihuahua of the genuine tweeter variety, who shook all over and bared his miniscule teeth if you so much as glanced in his direction. Buster belonged to my next-door neighbor Kenny's sister, Susie, and was actually not a bad little fellow once he'd sniffed you up and down. Then he'd jump in your lap and tremble violently, eventually mustering up enough courage to give you a tentative lick.

Truman's coming out occurred on a significant occasion: July 4—Independence Day in more ways than one. Susan and Kenny were having a big barbecue and I'd made the pizza buns and chicken. When I brought the food and Truman over, all hell broke loose. Truman took one look at Buster and went berserk, flinging himself at the poor dog and whimpering with something akin to mad passion.

"Isn't that cute?" Susie cooed.

But suddenly Truman attacked Buster from the rear, grabbing the astonished animal around the waist and humping him.

"*Real* cute," snorted Kenny, the ex–army sergeant.

"Oh, my God!" Susie gasped.

"You've got yourself a queer dog," Kenny observed.

"What's queer?" Matthew, Susie's eight-year-old son, wanted to know.

"Gay," said Michael, his ten-year-old brother. "Truman's gay!"

Well. Let me tell you, I knew just how Stan felt. Everybody was laughing, but it was laughter with a disturbed undercurrent. Nobody knew quite how to handle the situation. All Buster could do was shake and yelp while Truman carried on as merrily as if he were on a ride at Disneyland. But the more Buster struggled to free himself from Truman's clutches, the more ardent his pursuer became. Buster snarled and snapped, to no avail. He ran off and Truman followed him, tackling him in the hallway and climbing aboard for another go.

Eventually Buster became so rattled that he had to be put in another room. This made Truman *really* crazy. He ran to the cruel door that separated him from his beloved and emitted heartrending wails until Buster's muzzle could be seen peeking out from under the door. He was still snarling, a response that Truman evidently interpreted as a declaration of love, because he tried to lick Buster's nose.

"Hey!" said Kenny. "What part of *no* don't you understand, Truman?"

"I don't know what's gotten into him," I mumbled. "He's never done anything like this before." My stumbling apologies only elicited more laughter, so I scooped Truman up and carried him home. This, however, was not a good solution. Back on his own turf, Truman whimpered hysterically and ran all over, looking for Buster. After he'd searched the whole house in vain, he planted himself at the front door like Orpheus at the gate to the underworld, determined not to budge until he was finally reunited with his Eurydice.

And I, alas, was Cerberus.

"No, you are not going anywhere, young man," I said sternly. "You've embarrassed me enough for one day."

Truman's wails increased in intensity.

"Stop it! Buster didn't like what you did. He's not in love with *you!*"

The wails grew higher and higher in pitch. After a few minutes of this I caved in and went next door.

"Can I borrow Buster for a couple of hours?" I asked.

Susie obligingly brought Buster over, accompanied by a

very excited Matthew and Michael, who had appointed themselves his chaperones. I felt slightly guilty, as if Buster was a sacrifice being delivered up to Truman's altar. As soon as Truman saw the object of his affection, he threw himself at poor Buster as if they'd been apart for twenty years instead of twenty minutes.

"If Buster's really miserable, I'll bring him back," I promised.

But Buster soon clicked into dog-duty gear, running around the living room and lifting his leg at every turn. "Hey!" I yelled helplessly as he anointed my leather couch, my antique Mexican cabinet, and the leg of my Arts and Crafts drop-leaf table (all in the space of about thirty seconds). I was reminded of a stray cat who'd once adopted us and whom I'd named Radar because he was sonically tuned in to my cats' feeding time. One day Radar managed to accomplish his lifelong goal of getting inside my house, whereupon he raced through the premises like a trigger-happy terrorist, spraying everything in sight as I chased him, yelling at the top of my lungs. He was taking aim at my new laser printer when I corralled him.

"Buster just peed in your office!" announced Matthew.

"Uh-oh!" yelled Michael, as Buster galloped out of the office and into the bedroom. "Now he's doing it by the bed!"

Unfortunately, there wasn't much I could do except haul out the old Nature's Miracle and clean it up. It was either that or send Buster home and face an evening of Truman's wailing.

After awhile, thank God, the two of them settled down and began playing. Soon they were united in the common sport of cat-chasing, tearing after poor Rhonda, who, upon seeing that chihuahuas were rapidly multiplying, finally squeezed herself behind the washing machine and didn't come out until the next day.

When Buster eventually went home, Truman cried pitifully.

"It'll last awhile," Susie said. "Buster once had a little chihuahua he was in love with. A *girl*," she added pointedly. "When she went home he cried for almost two days."

"Two *days* of this?" I shuddered.

"It's a pain in the ass, isn't it?" she laughed.

This seemed to be the end of Truman's gay period, until one evening, some months later, when Buddy Boy came over to visit. The two of them played very nicely for most of the evening. Just as Joanna and her husband, Todd, were getting ready to leave, however, Truman mounted Buddy.

"Truman! Quit it!" I was mortified.

But Buddy didn't seem to mind. In fact, he stood there quite calmly, as if that sort of thing happened to him all the time.

"It's okay," Joanna assured me, totally cool about Truman's advances. "Buddy does it to anything. Girl dogs, boy dogs, the chair leg, your arm . . ."

"Any port in a storm!" Todd chimed in.

I felt much less embarrassed after that. If Buddy Boy, the most macho chihuahua I'd come across, could hump a guy, being gay in the dog world was obviously in.

"We ought to deck them out in leather and take them cruising down Santa Monica Boulevard," I commented dryly.

"No way!" said Todd, looking worried. After all, if we could dress our chihuahuas in bomber jackets, anything was possible.

"She's just kidding, honey!" Joanna reassured him.

Don't be too sure.

A Widow, a Chihuahua, and Harry Truman

Chapter 18

Time Out from Guilt

I've almost never looked back on my life and wished I had done things differently. What would be the use of it?

Guilt is one of those annoying aspects of grief that definitely wears a person down. It's a sneaky enemy, creeping around the nooks and crannies of the subconscious and surreptitiously eating away at good sense, which in mourning is already in a state of precarious vulnerability.

Harry Truman was famous for his immunity to the disease of hindsight. He always chose to look forward rather than back, refusing to succumb, as his devoted Secretary of State Dean Acheson observed, to "that most enfeebling of emotions, regret."

How often I wished, after Adam had died, that I could be more like Harry in this respect. But when we lose a loved one, no matter how wonderful the relationship might have been, there are always recriminations and regrets. In my case, although I knew logically that no one could have loved Adam more than I did, I was still beset by a postmortem tidal wave of should and shouldn't haves.

My husband was a quiet, gentle man who never asked for much, was grateful for what he had, and didn't believe in whining. While these virtues would be a blessing to any wife, they also made it difficult, at times, to second-guess his real thoughts and needs. And so, after he died, I found myself reliving moments in which—had I been a mind-reader or maybe just a tiny bit smarter—I might have been more sensitive to what Adam *wasn't* saying as much as to what he *was*.

The little things I wished I'd done! There were the times I was on deadline—no, a writer's obligations don't grind to a halt just because somebody's dying—and I'd take a break to check on Adam. I'd ask if there was anything he needed ("No, love, not a thing") and if he was okay ("Of course—you're here, aren't you?"). I'd take him at his word, give him a kiss, and go back to the computer, not realizing until after his death, when I had plenty of time to think about too many things, that he desperately wanted me to stop what I was doing and just be with him. But he was the sort of fellow who'd as soon swallow a box of tacks as interfere with my work.

And the hot summer night I had the fan on, not knowing he was chilled. When he finally asked me, in a soft voice, if I'd mind turning it off, I felt terrible. How could I have been so stupid, so thoughtless, as to forget that he was no more than skin and bones and it might as well have been winter as far as he was concerned?

It's indeed amazing what the human mind can concoct in the way of self-torment. Many were the nights I spent begging Adam's forgiveness for a whole roster of imagined sins that

A Widow, a Chihuahua, and Harry Truman

were no more than the inevitable oversights one commits in the course of daily life. It was as if I needed pardon for being human. Thank God, then, for all the books on loss that helped me to keep my sanity. Every one of them assured me that guilt is a normal part of the grieving process, from regretting the things we never got to do or say, to lamenting not having been able to save our loved one or prevent his or her death, to feeling blameworthy for simply being alive while he or she had to die.

But it was Truman who taught me a lesson that really put the whole guilt thing in its proper perspective.

One awful day, about a year after he'd been contentedly going to his sitter's, adolescence dealt their happy relationship a nearly irreparable blow.

The sad but inevitable fact was that Truman was growing up. Teenaging, actually. Suddenly I found myself facing those abominations all too familiar to parents of the puberty set: rebellion, assertion of identity, willful and wanton destruction of property, shameless disregard for the sensible rules that keep our hallowed social structure from crumbling into a helpless heap.

Understanding your teenage chihuahua, however, is perhaps even more bewildering than trying to get a bead on your teen son or daughter. First of all, while nature kindly puts us on the alert with the physical signs of approaching adulthood in humans, nothing in Truman's appearance indicated this momentous change. He was still the same six pounds, with the same heart-melting big brown eyes and innocent smile. His enormous bat ears were still two times too large for his head. In short, he didn't look a day over one. No wild growth spurts, no pimples, no changing voice, no sudden and inexplicable contempt for anyone over sixteen—in short, no clear warning signs that would have given me time to prepare myself for the dastardly upheaval that was just around the corner.

And so, what a shock it was to hear from Sant Kaur that Truman had, for no discernible reason whatsoever, gone berserk, doing his business all over the house.

I was mortified. How could this be? He *never* did that at home—not anymore, anyway. And he'd always been a model citizen at Sant Kaur's, obediently following the noble Missy's saintly example of canine do's and don'ts. But now, out of the blue, he was asserting himself with a vengeance.

And it wasn't as if he didn't know what he was doing. Sant Kaur said that when she'd discovered one of his presents on the floor and yelled, "*Who* did this?" the culprit was already slinking off, out of the living room and into the hallway designated as the "time-out" region for the pets when they were naughty. But this time Sant Kaur didn't even have to say the words; Truman went directly into the hallway corner and hid his head. Sant Kaur admitted that under the circumstances it was extremely difficult to keep a straight face. But she did her best to deliver a stern lecture.

"What did you say?" I asked.

"I asked him if he thought he was behaving like a gentleman. I told him he wasn't, and that his behavior was thoroughly unacceptable. I said that as long as he could act like a gentleman, he would be able to stay in other people's houses, but if he continued to act like this he wouldn't be welcome anywhere."

"And what did he do?"

"He just hung his head. He knew how bad he'd been."

But Sant Kaur's lecture, chilling as it was, didn't have the hoped-for effect. Truman apparently had decided that Marlon Brando was a far more appealing role model than Rex Harrison. The Wild One was not to be kept down. In the ensuing week, Truman pissed on Sant Kaur's bathrobe, on her down comforter, and, in the most defiant act of all, right inside her daughter's slipper.

That was the last straw.

"I don't know if we can continue to take him," Sant Kaur said to me when I went to pick up the juvenile delinquent. "I mean, we just can't have him doing this."

"My slipper was so cold and squishy," Amrit Sangeet complained. "Yuck!"

"Well, I hope you're happy," I scolded Truman on the way home. "You're a disgrace to me, you know that? Look at Missy. *She'd* never pee-pee or poo-poo in the house. The idea wouldn't even flicker across her consciousness. And now Auntie Sant Kaur doesn't want you back. This isn't funny, Truman. Do you understand?"

I'd read in a number of animal books with a metaphysical bent that you should never treat your pets condescendingly and should always talk to them as you would to your peers, respectfully, intelligently, just as if they understand every word you're saying. I thus made my words as pointedly serious as possible. But Truman only gazed up at me adoringly. Oddly enough, though, his eyes held a certain brightness indicative of comprehension. I felt a bit of a chill. He *did* understand. And he had no intention of mending his ways. His happy grin said, "I know just what I did. And I'll do it again!"

That was when it dawned on me that it was impossible to make him feel guilty because he had no idea of what guilt was. Like anger, guilt is a word that's not in the animal dictionary.

A dog might know that it's done something its owner doesn't like. But as far as feeling *guilty* about the act goes, forget it. Two minutes later it's history, and your pet is headed toward the future without so much as a backward glance at his reprobate past.

What an amazing thought—a world without guilt!

I let myself imagine what it would be like to release all the guilt I was carrying about Adam. Just pretend it was a pile of poop on the rug and nothing more. How would that feel?

Like taking off a ball and chain and running free, or throwing the cross on your back off a cliff and soaring straight to heaven. Good—damn good. So why was I doing this to myself? Did I really think I had to suffer because Adam had to suffer? The last thing he would have wanted was for me to be unhappy.

Suddenly it all seemed so ridiculous. I could be either miserable or not; the choice was mine. And I had chosen to tote the burden of guilt while any sensible animal would have unloaded it in a second. I looked at Truman with newfound admiration. If only we could trade brains, I'd probably be a whole lot better off. My therapist's words, "Has it ever occurred to you that that little chihuahua could be a guru in disguise?" floated back to me.

But if he *was* a guru, he was an incontinent one. When we got home I called the cats' sitter, Sharon Carter, an animal expert on whose advice I'd always relied.

"It's abandonment," was her prompt diagnosis.

"Abandonment? But I've taken him to Sant Kaur's a million times. He loves it there."

"But he's at that age where he's rebelling," she explained. "I think you've been taking him there too often. He misses you, and this is his way of letting everybody know that he's pissed. Literally."

"What am I going to do? Never go away again?"

"I'd suggest an animal behaviorist."

Oh, right. I'd met an animal behaviorist once, a nice woman I'd interviewed for my "Eccentric L.A." column in *L.A. Style* magazine. She specialized in going to people's homes and putting wayward pets on the path to redemption. Unfortunately, however, as we chatted in her living room, her own four pets—two big rottweilers and two jealous cats—refused to obey a single one of her commands, jumping all over the furniture (and me) as she helplessly pleaded, "Delilah, now stop that! Topaz, no!" It made for a great piece, but it didn't exactly make me a convert to pet therapy.

My friend Terry, who possesses an unerring insight into both human and animal nature, seemed to hit the nail on the head.

"He's angry that you've left him and he knows that peeing and pooping are powerful weapons. If Sant Kaur won't take him back, you'll be forced to be with him full-time. He'll have you to himself at last. So that's why he was smiling up at you when you yelled at him. His plan is working!"

Great. Here I was, the innocent victim of a chihuahua's careful plotting. I had the feeling that it wouldn't be long before Truman was beating me at chess.

It was then that I remembered Buddy Boy's pants. I called Joanna and asked if I could borrow his spare pair. Alas, she'd lost them, but she suggested a baby-clothes store.

"They're definitely the answer," she assured me. "The worst that can happen is he'll pee in the pants and go around wet. But he'll never want to do *that* again. Just keep the pants on when he's home alone and take them off and walk him as soon as you come back."

Now the only time I'd ever bought anything in a baby-clothes store was six years before, when I'd found a teeny-weeny little Scottish golfer's outfit for my then five-month-old nephew. As I've explained, I've never had either kids or younger siblings, so the entire world of babyhood is a big mystery to me. It was an even bigger mystery when I went to Macy's children's department, where all I could find in infant swimwear was tiny Tommy Hilfiger boxer trunks for thirty-two dollars.

"That dog is *not* getting Tommy Hilfiger trunks," I vowed before God.

"Pardon me?" said the sales clerk.

"Uh, listen. Don't you have any infant underwear?"

She looked at me with concern. "There's no such thing," she said.

"Why not?"

"Because they wear diapers."

Diapers! Why hadn't *I* thought of that?

"Thanks," I said, and sped off to Rite Aid. There I found shelves full of diapers for babies twelve pounds and up. I thought of that great scene from *Three Men and a Baby*, where a hapless Tom Selleck has to buy diapers for the first time in his life and comes back with ones that are three sizes too big. This time it was One Woman and a Chihuahua. These diapers definitely qualified as infant swimwear, because Truman would be swimming in them. At last, after meticulous searching, I found it: a bag of Newborn Huggies for babies ten pounds and under.

At the checkout counter, the clerk gave me the beneficent smile reserved for new mothers.

A Widow, a Chihuahua, and Harry Truman

"How much does your baby weigh?" she asked.

"He's seven pounds," I replied proudly. "He was six but he's getting fat."

"How cute! He must be brand new."

Excuse me, everybody, but I just couldn't resist this one. "Oh, no. Actually, he's two and half."

She looked distressed.

"Oh, he's very healthy and extremely bright," I assured her. Smiling sweetly, I walked off, leaving the poor woman swaying in the wind.

When I got home, the real fun began. The last time I had diapered anything was sometime in 1963, when at twelve years of age I'd been given the daunting job of babysitting the obstreperous one-year-old son of my mom's friend. Bear in mind that this unsuspecting woman had enlisted my services for just a few hours, completely unaware that I knew absolutely nothing about babies. As for my mother, I guess she'd forgotten what it was like to be infant-illiterate and just assumed that my natural mothering instincts would automatically click into gear.

Like Truman, little Scotty soon learned how easy it was to get me to jump to his commands. He began by throwing his toys out of his crib and crowing with glee as I ran to pick them up and put them back in the crib. I fetched for Scotty for about half an hour, at which point he began to cry. And cry, and cry.

I remembered that his mother had said he'd probably be thirsty and I should give him orange juice. So I poured some orange juice in a glass and handed it to Scotty, who looked justifiably bewildered.

"Here," I said. "It's juice. Drink it."

Scotty looked up at me questioningly. Then he grasped the glass in his two little hands and began to lap up the juice, like a dog. Soon it began to dawn on me that he was too little to drink like me and that I should have put the juice in a bottle. That's how hopeless I was.

But then, when Scotty began to scream again, I smelled the telltale signs of diaper-changing time.

Remember, dear reader, that this was way back in the Safety Pin Age, long before the dawn of Pampers. I studied the pile of diapers, the pins, and Scotty. Oh, well. It couldn't be *that* hard, could it? I took Scotty's diaper off—that was easy enough—and threw it in the wastebasket, not even knowing enough to empty its contents into the toilet, an odorous faux pas that I'm sure totally charmed his parents when they returned. Then I got a new diaper and tried to center Scotty on it. He responded by screaming and kicking, which made me freak out. I couldn't call my mother because she was out with Scotty's mom. So I did what I always did in an emergency: I called my genius of a twin brother.

David was short, fat, and the class brain. He had glasses, braces that made his mouth look like a metal factory, a high-pitched unchanged voice, and a brush-cut that sprouted from his round head like a soft lawn. There was absolutely nothing in his appearance to indicate that he should be any more of an expert in the fine art of diapering than I was. But David possessed two things I didn't: an extremely analytical mind and a cool head.

"Don't panic," he said over the phone. "Do you have baby powder?"

"What for?"

"You put it on the baby so he doesn't get diaper rash."

"Okay, yeah." I found the baby powder.

A Widow, a Chihuahua, and Harry Truman

"Now, first you clean him off."

I found a washcloth and wiped Scotty off.

"Now powder him."

It was amazing. As soon as Scotty sensed that I finally knew what I was doing, he calmed down and lay there very obligingly with his legs in the air.

David walked me through the remaining steps as if he did them every day, and that's how I diapered my first baby—and also, I'm sure, why I decided never to have any of my own.

And now here I was, decades later, about to make my second attempt. I read the directions on the Huggies; they said to put the baby on the diaper and secure the quilted tabs on either side of him. Could it possibly be simpler?

"Come here," I said to Truman, who jumped up on the couch. I laid him down on the diaper. He struggled and squirmed just as Scotty had, and I felt the eerie specter of déjà vu. But unlike Scotty, Truman was able to jump up and run off, which meant that I had to work fast. I fumbled with the tabs; Truman squirmed out of the diaper. I held him down and pulled the front of the diaper up and managed to fasten one side; he squirmed out again. I grabbed him, held him down, fastened one tab and then the other. There! Truman jumped up and the diaper slid down. Drat. I'd forgotten that Huggies didn't come with tail holes.

By this time Truman was hiding under the coffee table and absolutely refused to come out. So I took him to Sant Kaur's with Huggies in tow, and it actually took all three of us—Sant Kaur, Amrit Sangeet, and myself—to diaper him, mark the spot for the tail hole, cut the hole, and pull his tail through.

"I don't know if I want to go through this every day," Sant Kaur grumbled.

I don't blame her. So I'm now making a formal request to Huggies, for a line of diapers with tail holes. And the same goes for Tommy Hilfiger. If he comes out with some infant swim trunks with a tail hole, I just might break down and shell out the thirty-two bucks. After all, a chihuahua in Tommy trunks could qualify as art (by Warhol standards, anyway).

Chapter 19

Give Us This Day
Our Daily Rat

You get disgusted sometimes, and I certainly did,
when a man has a chance to make an orderly and pleasant
transfer and doesn't have sense enough to do it.

—*On Eisenhower's rudeness to him
on Inauguration Day, 1952*

With any new addition to a family, sibling rivalry is
bound to rear its ugly head. In the case of our household, it
soon became Petie versus Truman, and it made me thank God
a thousand times over that I'd never had kids. A mere cat and
dog were enough to send me to a padded cell.

The transfer of power wasn't a smooth one. The new potentate was in no way going to make life easy for the old one. Poor
Petie, who had always been the Golden Boy, was suddenly demoted to the status of beggar. Whenever he tentatively approached me for a stroke or two, Truman would throw himself

in front of enemy lines like a live blockade and push Petie back with his paws. Petie would retreat, hurt, whereupon I would come to the rescue, pick him up, and kiss him.

This drove Truman absolutely berserk. First he'd whine. Then, if I ignored him, he'd go into Phase Two and butt his head against my leg. If this strategy failed to produce results, he'd actually go into orbit, jumping as high as he could and trying to knock me down. Although it may seem ridiculous to even imagine a puny chihuahua toppling a full-size human, let's not forget David and Goliath. Truman's cleverness making up for what he lacked in size, the little brat would charge at the back of my knees, making them buckle every time.

When I'd finally put Petie down, Truman would attack him in a fit of jealousy, a kamikaze act that always ended in Petie's paw shooting out and smacking Truman on the nose. And then Mommy would have to pick her baby up and kiss the owie, and Truman would grin down victoriously at Petie from the exalted vantage point of my arms, practically sticking his tongue out in triumph. Tossing his head in disgust, Petie would saunter off, tail held high in the midst of temporary defeat. But his once-proud shoulders had an unmistakable droop, and my heart ached.

Things got so bad that I had to sneak around the ever-watchful Truman to give Petie fleeting moments of love on the sly. If Truman caught us en flagrante, the results were disastrous. He would wail and growl and pounce on Petie, who would usually flee from both of us and take a flying leap out the window. I worried constantly that one day he simply wouldn't come back.

The insanity reached a peak the night Petie, in a desperate attempt to gain the upper paw, brought in a lovely gift for me—a dead rat. This loathsome object, thoughtfully deposited smack in the middle of the living room, greeted me with four dead paws pointing heavenward. Thinking that it was a new toy, Truman made for it enthusiastically until I screamed, halting him in startled confusion. Petie ambled in at this moment and looked up at me with unabashed pride.

"Thank you, Petie." I picked him up, heroically resisting the urge to puke. "How sweet of you."

Truman watched all this jealously. Then, figuring out that the rat was the cause of Petie's promotion, he proceeded to grab it in his mouth and bring it over to me, as if some of the glitter might rub off on him.

"Truman! Get away from that thing!" I shrieked. Petie jumped out of my arms, shocked and offended. I ran into the bedroom and called my friend Terry in hysterics.

"There's a dead rat in my living room!" I sobbed, feeling like poor wheelchair-bound Joan Crawford in the memorable dinner sequence of *Whatever Happened to Baby Jane?* when her deranged sister (Bette Davis) served her a dead rat in a chafing dish.

Having four cats of her own, Terry was a veteran. "I know it's horrible," she said. "You just have to get a shovel."

"I don't *have* a shovel!" I wailed.

"Well, you'll have to use the broom and dustpan then. It's disgusting, but that's the price we pay for having these creatures."

And so it went. The fact that the cats have never really warmed up to Truman is all the more annoying when you consider that Rascal and Crystal, Sant Kaur's cats, are best pals with Truman. Many were the reports I'd received of happy goings-on as the three of them tore through the house playing tag or wrestled each other all over the floor. Of course, Rascal and Crystal had grown up with Missy and were comfortable with her. I'd even seen Rascal rubbing up under Missy's chin and licking her nose.

Needless to say, Truman was thoroughly confused when, after a trip to Sant Kaur's, he'd come back all wound up and ready to party, only to be greeted with hisses and flicking tails. He'd rush up to Rhonda, expectantly awaiting the invitation to play. Instead, Rhonda would arch her back, spit at him, and then look up at me, whining as if to say, "*Mom!* Do I *have* to?"

One morning something really funny happened. Truman was on the bed when he saw Petie ambling by. As the cat wandered past the bed, Truman took a flying leap and tackled him. Poor Petie looked as stunned as if he'd been Joe Montana ambushed by a midget junior-league linebacker. But he recovered enough of his composure to give Truman a venomous look and a good swat. Crestfallen, Truman crawled over to me for solace.

"Well, what do you expect, coming out from nowhere at Petie?" I lectured him.

But when I told Sant Kaur about it, she laughed heartily.

"Oh," she said, "he got that from staying with us. Tackle is Rascal's favorite game. That's where Truman learned it."

Once, after a trip to New York, I decided to leave Truman with Sant Kaur for an extra few days so that the cats and I could have some quality time. It almost broke my heart to see their joy. They hung around my legs, tripping me every time I took a step, following me from room to room and meowing to be picked up and held. They both cuddled up to me in bed, and Petie even held my hand in both his paws, claws firmly entrenched in case I entertained any ideas of running away again.

A Widow, a Chihuahua, and Harry Truman

But I don't think I got the full impact of their gratitude until I began receiving, every day, a token of their appreciation, in the form of a dead rodent.

It was the most amazing thing. Every morning I'd go outside and there it would be, in the same exact spot, the center of the driveway. It was either a mouse, a rat, or a gopher, and it was always laid out very carefully on its side, not simply flung over the shoulder with carefree abandon. Sometimes one of the cats would be stationed next to it, in order to make a personal presentation. Then I'd have to hide my revulsion and make a big display of gratitude. Once, when I was late in rising, Petie sat outside by the trophy, meowing stridently until I came down to thank him. He actually beamed, butting his head against me and purring so violently I thought he was going to have an orgasm.

When the two of them were safely out of sight, I'd tackle the nauseating problem of how to get rid of their gruesome gifts. If Susan and Kenny were home, I'd borrow their long-handled dustpan, sweep up the rat or mouse, and gingerly dump it in the vacant lot down the street. Sometimes I was lucky and my cleaning lady, Dora, who was my age but far more fearless, would dispose of the prize.

"Doesn't it make you sick?" I asked her.

"No," she said, shrugging. "Is dead. When they not dead and they run around"—here she imitated a scampering rat with her fingers—"Oooh! Then I no like. But if is dead is okay."

Another time Phil from across the street got my vote for the Prince Valiant Award for Bravest Man in the Neighborhood. I was having dinner guests, and of course the cats had picked this occasion to leave me not one but two fat rats, one in the usual sacrificial site and the other on the doorstep. Phil happened to be passing by at the moment of discovery and saw my consternation.

"Want me to get rid of them for you?" he offered.

"Would you? I've got a broom and a dustpan."

"Don't need 'em," he replied, picking up both rats by their tails. I thought I was going to pass out, but Phil just sauntered over to the huge ivy bed in front of his house and tossed the rats in as nonchalantly as if they were carrots going into a soup pot.

The whole thing fascinated me. I finally came to the conclusion that the cats were probably leaving ritual offerings to the Cat Goddess, who had finally answered their prayers to make that dog disappear forever. Or maybe *I* was the Cat Goddess, who knows? At any rate, their daily gifts continued to arrive until Truman came home, whereupon they abruptly stopped. Uh-oh. The Cat Goddess had put one over on them.

After a few days I jocularly remarked to Petie that I'd been missing my presents. "Where's my daily rat, Petie?" I asked, stroking him. "I haven't had one for four days now."

Petie blinked and swished his bushy tail. Then he loped off. And what do you know? When I went outside that afternoon, there was a big dead rat in the middle of the driveway.

Merest coincidence, you say? Well, I waited until a few rat-less days had once again passed. Then I tried the same thing on Rhonda. "You're such a good hunter, Rhonda," I cooed. "Bring Mommy a big rat today, okay?"

And sure enough, there it was in the driveway a few hours later.

So don't tell me that cats don't understand English. Or that they're not as devoted to you—in their own way—as dogs.

A Widow, a Chihuahua, and Harry Truman

They just have a different way of showing you they care. How do I love thee? Let me count the rats.

In closing, I thought I'd share with you a little something I made up.

THE CAT'S LORD'S PRAYER

Our father, who art in heaven,
Hallowed be thy mane,
Thy catnip come,
Thy will be done,
On earth as it is in cat heaven.
Give us this day our daily rat
And forgive us our trespasses
Onto other people's lawns and patio furniture.
Lead us not into trash cans
And deliver us from chihuahuas,
For thine is the kingdom and the power
And the glory forever.
Me-ow.

Chapter 20

Thoughts on Home

Wherever you are, that's home.

—*From a letter*
to Bess Truman

The October following the first anniversary of Adam's death, I decided to take a trip to North Carolina.

After I became a widow, invitations immediately came from friends and family to visit them and "get away," "try a change of scenery," "take your mind off things." I've always found that latter expression somewhat amusing, wondering how you take your mind off something, and if you do, where you end up putting it. It's not like taking your feet off the table, or removing a vase from one surface and setting it down somewhere else.

No, regardless of where you go, your mind seems to follow. You can't put it in the kennel or send it off to camp. You can't even lose it, although a lot of times you might think you have.

So, although I "got away" as much as I could, staying with

A Widow, a Chihuahua, and Harry Truman

my sister-in-law in Oakland, my brother and his family in Michigan, my friend Steven in San Francisco, I couldn't stop missing Adam. Couldn't thwart the grieving process by "doing a geographic," to borrow the old Alcoholics Anonymous expression, and trying to run away from the pain.

There are a couple of reasons in particular why traveling not only doesn't get your mind off widowhood but sometimes makes it even more unbearable. One is that you're often returning to places you and your husband visited together. When it comes to swift kicks in the stomach, there's nothing like memory to deliver the blows. There's that restaurant you both loved. There's the place you took that wonderful walk, holding hands and kissing like giddy teenagers. There's the Wal-Mart where you had the photos developed and bought each other silly cards. Pretty soon you're feeling so desolate that you figure you should have stayed at home, in bed, under the covers, with your dog and cats plastered against you. At least you wouldn't be so damn lonely.

Another reason that getting away can spell emotional disaster is that a lot of times you find yourself demoted, through the fault of nobody in particular and circumstances in general, to the painful status of third wheel.

No matter how wonderful my brother and sister-in-law were to me, for instance, I couldn't escape the fact that they were a couple, a unit. We used to be a foursome, David and Deb, Adam and I. But now I was single and adrift, and my sense of loss became even more acute. It wasn't that Dave and Deb excluded me; on the contrary, I'd never felt more welcomed or included by anybody. It was just that I so missed the little things they still shared—the tender looks, the laughter, the touch of a hand, the quick kiss—that I'd often end up excusing myself to go to the bathroom or take a nap so that I could escape behind a closed door to have a good cry on the lam.

I wondered if it would ever get any better. If I'd ever be able to be around couples again and be happy for them instead of sad for me. If I'd ever be able to return to the places Adam and I loved and be cheered instead of destroyed by the memories.

So I decided to visit my cousin Claire, because that trip, at least, would be memory-free. I had never been to North Carolina, where she and her husband, Mike, had moved a couple of years before. I had never met Casey and Cider. There would be no ghosts to dodge, no traces of Adam to wipe away. It was brand-new territory, a chance to start a new scrapbook of memories that just might herald my moving on.

The only problem was that I couldn't bring Truman. Our plan was to spend a couple of days at Claire and Mike's house outside Raleigh, and then drive up to the famous Blue Ridge Mountains, where they'd rented a house for the weekend on spectacular Lake Lure—and where dogs were not allowed. Claire was afraid to leave little Truman alone with his cousins; their sitter came in only twice a day, to feed and walk them, and we didn't want to take a chance on what might or might not happen to a petrified chihuahua twenty-five hundred miles from home and at the mercy of two strange dogs.

So, regretfully, I took Truman to Sant Kaur's and ended up missing him dreadfully.

It was great, though, to see Claire and Mike and to meet Cider and Casey, two gorgeous golden retrievers (bred from champions) who were so graciously obedient it made me want to scream. It was just too bad Truman couldn't be there. A week in the company of his model-citizen cousins would undoubtedly have done wonders for *his* behavior.

A Widow, a Chihuahua, and Harry Truman

"He's still a puppy," Claire said soothingly. "He'll grow into a son you can be proud of, honey. Take an experienced mother's word for it."

Since that was what I'd heard from everybody, I had to trust that it was true. But the day I woke up to find Truman kowtowing to my commands still seemed about as far off as the Milky Way.

Claire and Mike lived in a beautiful Colonial-style home with skylights and cathedral ceilings and a nature preserve for their backyard. As I walked along a placid stream, on a dirt path carpeted with bright autumn leaves, I found myself longing for a home like theirs—for a home, period. Adam had been dead more than a year, and I had moved to an area I loved. Yet I still felt like an immigrant uprooted from her native land, trying to get her footing in a strange new world where solid ground constantly gave way to shifting sand.

My cousins were wonderful hosts. They took me on a grand tour of Raleigh, treated me to the best restaurants, gave me a guest bedroom and bath with all the trimmings. Then, as planned, they drove me up to Lake Lure, a breathtakingly beautiful body of water surrounded by majestic mountains dazzlingly attired in their fall finery. We had a wonderful house right on the water. During the day we glided along the lake on a pontoon boat, or took the elevator to the top of famous Chimney Rock, or toured the charming little nearby towns, stopping now and again for fresh apple cider at one of the many friendly roadside stands along the way. At night we'd sit around the fireplace, logs crackling and spitting sparks, and laugh ourselves silly or, since it was nearly Halloween, do the Ouija Board and scare ourselves silly. The two of them did their level best to give me the perfect vacation.

But I missed Adam. *Oh,* how I missed him. I felt, again, the old rage at having been cheated. My husband and I should have had ten years together like Claire and Mike. There should have been *four* of us in that cozy, romantic getaway overlooking the magnificent lake, curled up by the blazing fire, talking and laughing while the full moon beamed down at us from the star-studded sky, the water lapped peacefully at the dock below, and the cries of the loons pierced the evening stillness.

When I got to feeling too sorry for myself, I'd give myself a Truman dose. I had brought along *Dear Bess,* a book of fifty years of Harry Truman's letters to Bess Truman; and at night, in bed, I'd read it and try to get inspired by Harry's indefatigable energy, his uncanny ability to concentrate on the job at hand, even though he often felt empty without his beloved around. For much of her husband's tenure in Washington, both as senator and as president, Bess was an absentee wife, preferring to live quietly in Independence; and Harry bore it gracefully, even though you could tell that the one place he most wanted her to be was by his side.

Something he said in one letter particularly hit home.

June 10, 1946

Dear Bess,

Well, I miss you terribly—no one here to see whether my tie's on straight, or whether my hair needs cutting. . . .

I knew just how he felt. There was no one in my house now to care about the little, seemingly inconsequential details that make up a life. But the big difference was that Adam was dead and Bess wasn't. She was always there, at the other end of the phone or in the daily mail. She was alive and waiting, at the old house that would welcome Harry when he finally went home for good, to his beloved Independence, the old house that would be there forever, long after they both were gone.

So it wasn't the same. Harry had a home and I didn't. He had once written to Bess, "If you weren't there I couldn't go on." Maybe he wasn't such a pillar of strength after all. Maybe he would have fallen apart if she'd died, and felt angry and even, yes, sorry for himself. Maybe I didn't need to live my life by what I imagined to be his rules, because no matter how great he was, he was human just like me. It was something to think about, anyway.

Before I left North Carolina, Claire took me to an amazing watering hole in Raleigh by the name of the Black Dog Café.

The Black Dog was every canine obsessive's dream: an entire restaurant devoted to dogs. There were dog stuffed animals and dog sweatshirts and T-shirts and mugs for sale, along with toys, accessories, feeding bowls, gourmet treats—you name it. Dog posters adorned the walls. There were racks full of dog greeting cards. And the entire back room had been transformed into a photo gallery, where hundreds of patrons had pinned or pasted up a snapshot of their pet pride and joy.

There were dogs in hats and sunglasses, dogs performing and snoozing, dogs sporting the latest Halloween costume. Claire showed me where she'd put up a photo of Cider and Casey, looking incredibly dignified among the rabble. It was my golden opportunity—the reason, obviously, that God had sent me to Raleigh. I took out one of Truman's two passport photos and snagged one of the few remaining spaces. When I stood back to survey it, I was reassured that my baby was the cutest dog on the whole wall.

Claire was delighted. "Now whenever we come here, we'll see you and Truman."

After an extremely top-heavy meal of greasy hamburgers and onion rings that belonged in a shelter for battered foods, we were ready to leave when the chef appeared at our table. He was a big, friendly black man with a stomach that preceded him by approximately a mile.

"Ah am your chef," he said with great authority. "Mah name is Yancy, and ah am here to serve you. You know, chefs today forget that little fact, that our job is not just to create but to serve. Now, is there anything else ah can get for you?"

We shook our heads and thanked him.

"How was everything?"

"Just great," I assured him. "This is my first trip to North Carolina, and I wanted to taste some authentic regional dishes."

"Did you try mah bahbecue?"

"No."

"You didn't try mah bahbecue?" Yancy was incredulous. "You sit right there. Don't you move, now." He rushed back to the kitchen and returned with a small plate full of pork barbecue and a roll. My stomach lurched.

"Ah don't mind tellin' you that ah make the best bahbecue you'll ever taste," said Yancy modestly. "Ah have cooked everywhere in this country, from San Francisco to Lou'siana, Texas, Arkansas. Ah paint, you know. With food. And ah love to paint different pictures. So ah know mah Texas bahbecue, mah Lou'siana bahbecue, mah North Ca'lina bahbecue. And this is the best. You want to know the secret?" He bent down and whispered in my ear, "Vinegar! And pepper. Lots of pepper. Now go ahead. Eat up."

He left us and I took a taste. Unfortunately, on a full stomach, the effect of Yancy's palette on my palate was not entirely positive.

"What are you going to do?" Claire asked, convulsing in giggles.

"We're going to tell Yancy that this bahbecue is so good we have to share it with your husband, who's a bahbecue fanatic," I said. "Then we're going to wrap it up, take it home, and give it to Cider and Casey."

Yancy beamed when I complimented him. "Now," he said. "Have you tried mah gumbo?"

I thought Claire would fall off her chair. Yancy ran off and returned with a bowl of his gumbo. This time he watched as I took a bite.

"Ah've made gumbo everywhere," he reminisced. "But this here gumbo, now it's the best. You've got your chicken, your crab, your shrimps, your sausage . . ."

"It's wonderful, Yancy." I rose and shook his hand, determined to beat it before he brought out the rest of the menu. "And this is a great place. All dogs."

"Yep. You got a dog?"

"Oh, yes. Would you like to see his picture?"

"Certainly." Yancy was all Southern Gentleman. I led him into the back room and proudly pointed to Truman's photo on the Dog Wall of Fame.

"Well, now, isn't he something!" Yancy clucked. "What is he?"

"A chihuahua."

"One of them little things, huh? My, my. Will you look at those ears! What's his name?"

"Truman. After the President."

"Sure, sure. He was okay, Harry Truman. Okay."

As I stood at the photo wall at the Black Dog, I felt a curious kind of peace. There was something comforting about pinning Truman's photo on that wall, something that seemed to cut the world down to family-size. Somewhere twenty-five hundred miles away I knew that there was a piece of him, and myself, that I could always return to, and a piece of us that others could share. Claire would see us whenever she went back to the Black Dog, and it would feel, for a brief moment, as if I were there with her and time and space were no longer barriers to closeness.

I realized that I needed to leave markers now, thumbtacks here and there on the map of the rest of my life, which would give me the sense of connectedness for which I desperately yearned. Was that why astronauts left mementos on the moon, or tourists carved their names in the stones of distant lands—not merely to state to the world, "I was here," but to make the universe seem less vast and impersonal, to extend the boundaries, physical and psychological, of that mysterious place called home?

And so, on the day that Claire called me with the sad news that the Black Dog had suddenly and inexplicably closed, I felt a curious sense of loss. The Black Dog was far more than just a restaurant I had visited once. It was a symbol of the new roots I was trying to put down, the roots that death had destroyed and memory would rebuild.

A Widow, a Chihuahua, and Harry Truman

I mourned its loss. But its departure reminded me, once again, of the futility of relying on material things to give us our sense of identity and place. In the beautiful film *The Trip to Bountiful*, the late great actress Geraldine Page, in her final role, plays a restless, querulous old woman who is convinced that if she can just get back to her childhood home, she'll once again be happy. Overcoming a variety of obstacles, she makes the tedious, difficult journey on a Greyhound bus to the place that memory has kept young, only to discover an abandoned, tumble-down shack, imprisoned in an overgrowth of weeds, that is teetering, like her, on the brink of death. She sees, then, that home isn't a physical place but a place of satisfaction within the self, and that when we find that place—be it through our work, or art, or relationships, or religion—we'll *always* feel at home, no matter where the winds of destiny may take us.

Adam's death caused me to reexamine the entire notion of *home*. I looked it up in the dictionary; its German root, *heim*, means "base," though its many definitions encompass everything from the city, state, or country in which one lives to "the place where one finds satisfaction" and even "the grave." Over and over I asked myself what elements made up home for me. And gradually, as the months passed, I saw that the more at home I felt with myself, the more I felt at home, regardless of where I was. I didn't need Adam, or anyone, to give me a home; I could give that to myself, by living at full creative, artistic throttle.

Today I would say that home, for me, is where my writing is. Writing is what makes me happy, gives me a sense of true fulfillment, connects me to myself and others. My writing puts down strong roots and bears pungent fruits; it helps me to see, hear, and feel more acutely, so that I'm more passionately and compassionately attuned to life. It touches people I know, in ways that delight me, and people I don't, in ways I couldn't imagine, spinning a sort of invisible web that catches hearts and souls and helps me to feel that I'm never alone.

Where is *your* home? Is it where you live? Where your family lives? Do you have a "dream home," a place in either the future or the past that you imagine holds the secret to your happiness? Is home where your heart is? Or where your spirit is?

Wherever your home is, I hope that you find it, or that it finds you.

Chapter 21

Remembering Harry

Harry Truman never learned how to put on a public face, and he never had a public manner. He just never learned how to be anybody except himself.

—Judge Albert A. Ridge

As anyone who's lost a spouse knows, anniversaries are hell. Like cranky customs officers at the border, they're always there, ready to stop you, search you, question you, and—if they have any say about it—prevent you from crossing over to the other side of grief. You can spend months pulling yourself together and thinking you're getting better, but the anniversary police will always be up ahead, waiting to send you back to the jail of despair, daring you to get on with your life.

As what would have been Adam's and my fourth anniversary approached, I was filled with sadness and apprehension. How was I going to get through it? Having graduated from the magical-thinking stage of grief, I didn't want to revisit one of our favorite places and try to pretend he was with me again. Neither did I want to be with my family; our anniversary had been such a special day, reserved for just us two, that I couldn't quite imagine sharing it with anyone but Adam.

But then, as often happens on this unpredictable trip we call life, fate made me an offer I couldn't refuse.

My best friend, Steven, a telecommunications exec for Bank of America, was going to a conference at a ritzy hotel in Palm Springs and invited me to spend a few days in paradise with him, on the house. "I'll be at seminars all day," he said. "You'll be on your own; you can relax, get some writing done, do whatever you want." It seemed like the ideal solution—I could be by myself during the day and have Steven's company in the evening. It would be a new environment, an adventure. I couldn't think of a single good reason to say no.

The Renaissance Esmeralda was one of those posh resorts most of us never expect to enter, let alone for free. When we pulled in to the massive circular drive in front of the hotel, I was suitably awed. This place was a veritable palace. Enormous entranceways, lobbies, and anterooms with inlaid-marble floors greeted us as we walked in. I couldn't count the number of fountains, inside and out, not to mention the number of chandeliers. The lobby had a row of exclusive shops and a complete business center with computer workstations. A splendid carved cherrywood spiral staircase with giant marble globes at either end led from the lobby level down to the terrace, where there were four restaurants. Outside were Grecian pools and waterfalls, a complete fitness spa, two Jacuzzis, and two eighteen-hole golf courses (just in case one was out of order, I suppose).

The real kick was the elevators. Each one was fashioned of carved cherrywood, with a chandelier, tapestries on two of the walls, and a plush embroidered Chinese rug that read "Have a nice Sunday." I checked my watch; it was indeed Sunday. The following morning, when I stepped into the elevator, the rug greeted me with "Have a nice Monday." Seven separate rugs, one for every day of the week? Why not?

Our room had a balcony overlooking the Grecian pools, with a breathtaking view of the surrounding mountains. It also had three phones, one of which was in the bathroom, along with an extra TV, in case you were in the middle of your favorite program when nature called. At yet this, I discovered, was one of the low-end accommodations, at a paltry 350 dollars a night.

I'm not ashamed to say that for three spectacular days and nights I shed all of my liberal-proletariat pretensions and became bosom buddies with Decadence. I ate like a pig; I lay by the Grecian pools, with the sound of the waterfall crashing around me, and gazed up at an azure sky or at stars blazing bright as the Vegas Strip at midnight; and I pretended that I was rich enough to be there on my own. The only thing that was missing was Truman. Not only did I miss the little bugger, but he was the kind of dog for whom the Esmeralda was built. I fantasized about walking him through the stately halls on his red-and-gold embroidered leash, dressed in his little red turtleneck, in true filthy-rich Palm Springs matron style. My *dear!*

One morning I wandered into Z. Klein, the resort's exclusive jewelry store. It looked like the kind of place whose doors you'd be afraid to darken without eight hundred thousand dollars in spending money, but I was feeling bold. At the doorway of Z. Klein lay a tiny white poodle, in a light-blue harness with a royal-blue leash, just like Truman's.

"And who's this?" I inquired, stooping down to pet the poodle, who opened its sleepy eyes and began licking my arm off.

"That's Baby!" beamed a small, nice-looking older gentleman.

"She's our pride and joy," added the slender, handsome woman standing next to him.

"I have a chihuahua," I said, "with a harness and leash in those exact colors."

Dog fashion being an exciting topic of conversation in these parts, I soon found that I'd made two new friends. The little man, Mr. Klein, was a charming fellow with a cultivated Eastern European accent. His companion and partner, Nancy, had a gentle Arkansas drawl full of genuine warmth. My ever-reliable sixth sense told me that these two discerning individuals would appreciate Truman's passport photo.

"Oh, Zoltan, she has a picture of her chihuahua!" Nancy poked him excitedly. "Isn't he adorable?"

"Oh, my, he *is* cute!" Mr. Klein nodded admiringly. "What's his name?"

"Truman. After Harry Truman, my idol."

"You have very good taste," Mr. Klein complimented me. "He was a wonderful president. Too bad it took thirty years for the rest of the world to come to the same conclusion."

"He was so *real*," mused Nancy.

"The salt of the earth," added Mr. Klein. "We went to his house, you know."

"In Independence?"

"Yes. And it was so unassuming! His old coat was still on the rack. He was the most ordinary man!"

"Not ordinary," I said. "Humble, but anything but ordinary."

"You're right. There was no one else like him."

"Where are you from, Mr. Klein?" I asked.

A Widow, a Chihuahua, and Harry Truman

"Hungary."

"My family was from Austria and Yugoslavia," I told him. "They had to come over in 1938. They just escaped the Holocaust."

"I came here after the war," Mr. Klein said. "But I wasn't fortunate enough to escape the Holocaust. I was in Auschwitz. And Buchenwald."

"I'm so sorry," I said awkwardly.

Mr. Klein shrugged. "After the war I went to Italy. I was young, fifteen years old. I apprenticed to a master jeweler. I learned my trade. Look, let me show you something."

He led me to one of the glass jewelry cases and pointed to some of the most exquisite pieces I'd ever seen. Golden peacocks with jewel-studded plumes, delicate butterflies with intricately carved wings, a three-dimensional diamond rose whose petals were fashioned with hundreds of tiny stones that sparkled so brightly you almost had to shield your eyes. All of them were designed by Mr. Klein, and painstakingly hand-crafted.

"How much is that rose, Mr. Klein?" I asked.

"Fifteen thousand dollars," he replied. Noticing that he'd put me into shock, he added, "These are fifty-eight-faceted diamonds, each one inlaid by hand. Do you know what a fifty-eight-faceted diamond is?"

I shook my head.

"Look." Mr. Klein invited me to inspect the piece through his jeweler's glass. I gasped as each magnified diamond seemed to shoot sparks of fire.

Later that afternoon, when I brought Steven, who was an art history expert, in to see Mr. Klein's creations, he was overwhelmed.

"I just saw the exhibit of the Romanoff jewels in San Diego," he said to Mr. Klein. "These pieces are comparable to many of those."

"Of course," Mr. Klein agreed, nodding. "After all, we're talking about art."

I spent a couple of hours chatting with Mr. Klein. His wife, like my husband, had died of cancer, and he himself was undergoing chemo for bone cancer.

"Mr. Klein," I said, "tell me something. How do you live through it? How did you live through your wife's cancer, and how are you living through your own?"

Mr. Klein smiled and shook his head. "Who knows? You just do. You go day by day." He patted Nancy's hand. "But this lovely lady helps. And of course, Baby." He looked down lovingly at the poodle. "Dogs can give life meaning. Isn't that true, Baby?"

"How do you live with the memories of the concentration camps?"

Mr. Klein sighed. "You don't. You learn not to think about them."

He paused. "You know, if it weren't for Harry Truman, I wouldn't be here. He opened the doors to Jewish immigration after the war. Yes, your Truman is named after the right man."

Mr. Klein's fortitude put my own anniversary blues in perspective. If he could survive the concentration camps and the horrible memories they spawned and live a full life, and then continue to live a full life even after he'd buried his wife and found himself battling the same disease that had killed her, well, hell. I decided I could make a stab at being happy too. Or if not happy, at least grateful, for the terrible things that had never happened to me, and the wonderful things, like Adam, that had.

My husband's cousin by marriage, Eva Slott, smiled approvingly when I showed her Truman's photo. She, too, was a refugee from Hungary who had lost her family in the Holocaust.

"If it weren't for Harry Truman, I wouldn't be here," she said, in an eerie echo of Mr. Klein. "It was he who allowed all the postwar immigration. I came in December of 1947, and his was the first American election I experienced, in 1948. I remember going to sleep with a heartache, thinking Dewey was the next president, and waking up to find out it was Harry Truman. Oh, I was so happy! He was a wonderful man. He had—how do you say?—his head on straight, you know? He wasn't impressed by money or important people. I always had the feeling you could sit right down with him at the kitchen table, over a cup of coffee. He seemed like that kind of man."

It's really a curious thing, but through Truman the chihuahua, a verbal portrait began to emerge for me of Harry Truman. It wasn't your standard portrait, thoughtfully painted by historians, family, or friends; rather, it reminded me of a free-form collage, spontaneously fashioned out of bits and pieces of the memories of a broad spectrum of Americans, of all backgrounds and ages. Whoever met my Truman, or saw his photo, seemed to have some sort of reminiscence or opinion about the man after whom my dog was named.

In 1952, for instance, my friend Mickey Cottrell, who was then eight years old, had organized a protest against Harry Truman.

"He'd fired MacArthur!" Mickey explained. "Douglas MacArthur was the idol of every little boy in America. I mean, it was like firing God. So I got all the kids in the neighborhood to picket against Truman. We marched up and down Glenmar Street in Monroe, Louisiana, with signs that read, 'Truman's wrong! MacArthur's great!'"

But just as he did with history, Harry managed in the end to win Mickey over.

"Two years later I was in downtown Little Rock, Arkansas, when a big parade turned the corner. I didn't know what was going on; I'd just come downtown with a friend to see a movie.

"And then I saw Harry Truman, standing up in this green Cadillac convertible and waving. It was a monumental moment for me, since he was the first President I'd ever seen in the flesh. I remember that he was wearing a Panama straw hat and a string tie, and he had the greatest smile. So incredibly endearing. I immediately melted and forgave him. I'll never forget that smile."

"How do I remember Truman?" my mother mused. "Well, he was very likable. He had no pretensions. We liked his feistiness. And we loved him for his devotion to Margaret. That letter he wrote to that critic who panned her debut recital—we thought it was adorable.

"Margaret was a good scout. She was very sweet. And I don't think there was a president's daughter who was ever as well known. I remember her on TV. She did a routine with

A Widow, a Chihuahua, and Harry Truman

Jimmy Durante; it was very cute. She had a hat and a cane, and she said, 'My father'll kill me for this!'

"I remember somebody—maybe it was his mother—once said, 'Harry always planted the straightest row of potatoes.'"

One of my dearest friends is Sister Janet Harris, a nun who's worked in detention ministry for the last twenty-five years. Jan is like a vision—slender, serene, beautiful—only her silver-gray hair suggesting her age of almost seventy. But this soft-spoken woman worked in the trenches with L.A. gangs, and you definitely wouldn't want to tangle with her when her fighting Irish is up.

I'll never forget the time she and I went to the women's prison in Chino, California, where we were co-facilitating a class in spiritual journal-writing. The guard at the desk wouldn't let us in because someone had forgotten to put our names on the list. With her usual calm, Sister Jan asked to speak to the watch captain.

"He's not here," the guard replied.

"Where is he?" Janet asked sweetly.

"At home."

"I see." Janet smiled. "Well, you phone him this minute, and you tell him that Sister Janet is here and that if he doesn't give you the okay to let us in to teach our class, I'm going to wring his frigging neck!"

This little speech was delivered in her softest nun tone of voice. I wish I had a picture of the guard's face, with his mouth dragging on the floor. Needless to say, he got on that horn and called the watch captain, and two minutes later we were inside those prison walls.

"Sometimes that Sister Dear nonsense has just got to go," Jan explained nonchalantly.

Since Jan is one of my favorite people, I suppose it was inevitable that she'd be high on Truman's list as well. The first time he saw her, he went crazy, whimpering and dancing around her with more than his usual gregariousness. Janet picked him up and blessed him on the spot.

"May Mother Mary and all the dog angels watch over you, Truman," she intoned. "And may you bring Mary Beth lots and lots of joy."

One evening, at dinner, after Janet had returned from her first trip to Paris, she said, "You know, the thing about Truman is his purity of action. He's not like other dogs. He won't connive. He won't beg. Not like the dogs in Paris! When I was in a Parisian café I felt a sudden weight on my leg. I looked down and this dog had his head in my lap and was looking up at me with these eyes—charming, ingratiating, so *French!* But Truman isn't like that."

"Oh, yeah?" I snorted. Obviously she'd forgotten the dinner hour at my house, the signal for Truman to position himself on top of the couch next to the dining-room table, wistful eyes following each morsel of food as it traveled from plate to fork to mouth. "You know, that dog *has* to have his way."

"Oh, he's willful; I agree. But so was Harry Truman. He must have been willful. He *must* have. To do what he did, believe in himself and the truth, no matter what.

"There's a Zen saying I read," she continued. " 'Once you tell a lie, it's always repeated as the truth.' Harry Truman never lied. And as a result, he never played it safe. He always risked the truth. I never got the feeling that he was thinking about his ego. He was interested only in doing his job with the most integrity possible."

Casey Cohen, a dear friend of Sister Janet's, is one of the country's leading experts on juvenile justice and the death penalty, and for many years he's served as a consultant to high-profile defense attorneys. Tall, good-looking, with a gray beard and piercing eyes, Casey is one of those totally unselfaggrandizing people who are simply dedicated to the cause of justice. He has a biting sense of humor and a quiet, dry view of the world. Sister Janet says that Casey's distinguishing feature is his integrity, and that in all the years she's known him, he's never compromised his principles, not once. Definitely a Harry Truman type of guy.

Casey came to a party at my place one night, and when he met Truman (who had appointed himself the official host and was going from guest to guest, paw extended in welcome), he got pretty excited, for Casey. It turns out, with wondrous synchronicity, that once upon a time Casey had had both a cat and a dog named Truman.

"But not after Harry," he said. "After a drive-in restaurant in L.A. in the fifties. Truman's was the kind of place that doesn't exist anymore, where the guys would all drive up and eat and check out girls. Well, I found a cat at Truman's, so I named it Truman. Then the cat died and I got a dog, and I named the dog Truman. It just seemed like a good name."

Since in addition to his legal expertise, Casey also happens to be one of those political history whizzes who would have made you feel like the class retard, his seemed the perfect brain to pick about Harry Truman.

"Do you remember Truman?" I asked.

"*Remember* him? Hell, I precinct-walked for *Roosevelt!* That's how far back I go."

"But you're not *that* old, Casey."

"Thanks, kid. I was ten when Roosevelt died. I'd never heard another word go with 'President' except 'Roosevelt.' He'd been in office since before I was born. I mean, I was ten years old before I knew that 'Presidentroosevelt' wasn't one word. When I heard 'President Truman,' I was shocked."

Casey stretched his legs, enjoying his trip down Memory Lane.

"When I was twelve or thirteen, I was a politically astute kid. My daily reading consisted of the *New York Times,* the *Wall Street Journal,* the *Unesco Courier,* the *L.A. Times,* and the *Daily Mirror.* And I listened to the news—all the time. My first vivid memory of Harry Truman was listening to him on the radio when he announced the dropping of the atomic bomb. I thought it was great. You know, ten years of anti-Japanese propaganda had done its work. The war was all I knew, and anything that would end it was great.

"Truman was the most unlikely person to become president. I mean, he got his fame from spearheading this committee to ferret out Defense Department overspending during the war. Now the war was a great boondoggle for the Defense Department, who used it as a distraction to engage in a wild spending spree. So it took enormous integrity for Truman to do this.

"I want to tell you one thing that the history books *won't* tell you, and that's how incredibly vicious and relentless the vilification of Truman was in 1950, 1951, 1952. Potsdam was supposed to be a sellout to the Commies. You have to remember: here's the most powerful country in the world, and things are falling apart. It couldn't have just *happened*; there had to be corruption. So ninety percent of the newspapers carped on Truman, daily. It was worse than anything Clinton has endured. Truman was painted as a corrupt graft-monger; the cartoons were absolutely ruthless. Well, today all these old people will tell you how wonderful Harry Truman was—outspoken, honest, the best. But they were the ones who were pounding the nails into him in the early fifties.

"I remember the election of '48, sure. Nobody expected Truman to win. He was going all around campaigning on this train and stopping under every tree. We all thought it was funny. But damned if he didn't beat out Dewey."

And then there was the fabulous story that Jane Pasaden, a friend of my agent's, told me, about her mother's deathbed confession.

Theirs was a dyed-in-the-wool Republican family. Going off with a Democrat would have been the equivalent of a mixed marriage, said Jane. And so, naturally, when the election of 1948 rolled around, her mother's vote was taken for granted. Dewey had that precinct sewn up.

Well, many years later, when Jane's mother was dying, she gathered her children around her and said that she had something to get off her chest. It had haunted her for decades; she had to come clean.

Nobody could imagine what it was. Had she had an affair? Embezzled money? Killed someone?

"I voted for Harry Truman in 1948," she whispered. "I never told your father. I never told anyone."

Wouldn't Harry have loved *that* one! For who better than he knew what courage it sometimes takes to abandon the party line and follow your heart?

And so, with everyone I talked to, I learned a little more about Harry Truman, and about his effect on the American psyche. What came through the most was his integrity; his refusal to pretend to be anything more, or anything less, than exactly what he was. That seemed to really stick with people. Harry may not have been fully appreciated while he was in office, but today he shines like a beacon of hope, a symbol of purity in an unclean world. In fact, everybody wants him back, most of all me.

I was grateful for the many insights I got about Harry through people who had admired him. But I still longed to encounter someone, anyone, who had actually *known* him. Little did I know that a wild Hollywood Halloween party would be the vehicle the angels would choose to make my dream come true.

Chapter 22

Truman's Halloween

Truman had the knack of making the people he met feel that
he was truly glad to see them—and he usually was.

—*Charles Robbins in* Last of His Kind

Halloween in L.A. is the equivalent of a national holiday. It looks for all the world like a horrorized Christmas,
with trees festooned in bright orange lights, once respectable
lawns turned into tombstone-studded cemeteries, life-sized
witches and plastic rats, with glowing orange eyes, popping out
of bushes, and shrouds of cotton cobwebs hanging from the
houses like grisly flocking. People start dressing up and parad-
ing around days before the actual event, although in this town
I always wonder how the hell anybody can tell the difference.

My favorite coffeehouse, for instance, regularly caters to a
youthful clientele sporting everything from purple pineapple
hairdos to black lipstick, white makeup, and blinding clothes
reminiscent of the heady days of glam rock. It was at this very
hangout, in fact, that I ran into my hairdresser, Michael, his

boyfriend, Anthony, and their chihuahua, Max, the day before Halloween.

There was an admiring crowd around Max, and I soon discovered why. He was all dressed up as a tiny dragon, in a green felt costume complete with felt dragon scales and a little felt dragon-head hood.

"*Where* did you get that outfit?" I gasped.

"Michael made it," Anthony said proudly.

Michael grinned. "Had some extra time on my hands, ya know."

No, I didn't know. I'd failed sewing in my seventh-grade home-ec class, to the enormous chagrin of my Viennese grandmother Leontine Gersten, who had studied clothing design in Paris and was one of the top dressmakers in Rochester, New York.

"How I get granddaughter who cannot even thread needle?" she would muse in wonder, befuddled by a mystery only God could solve. But Michael, the granddaughter Leontine should have had, had not only designed Max's costume; he'd sewed the whole thing by hand.

"Ah, it was nothin'," he said, shrugging modestly.

Max looked so adorable—you could see only his little nose poking out from under the dragon head—that I decided Truman had to have a Halloween costume too. All I had was his bomber jacket and red knit scarf, but it would do in a pinch.

But where could we go to be admired? Oh, we could stroll the avenues, of course, collecting appreciative oohs and ahs, but that seemed too tame. Truman really deserved a *party*. Fortunately, my friend Steven, who was down from San Francisco for the weekend, came to the rescue. A gay friend of his was having a combination Halloween/fiftieth-birthday bash, which meant that every queen in West Hollywood would be there in full regalia. It was perfect!

The only problem was that traveling to West Hollywood on Halloween Eve is the equivalent of trying to drive into New Orleans on Mardi Gras. I knew we'd regret our destination as soon as we got in the car. The freeways were jammed and the surface streets, half of which were blocked off for the big Halloween parade, were so congested that what should have been a twenty-five-minute drive from my house turned into a one–and–a–half hour nightmare that rivaled Godard's *Weekend* for existential gridlock.

We finally arrived at our destination, nerves destroyed. Truman was already in a fragile state when we made our entrance. But when a roomful of wildly costumed revelers erupted in ecstasy at the sight of a doe-eyed chihuahua who looked as if he were about to join Snoopy in a Red Baron sortie, the poor dog freaked out and dove into my armpit. A chubby man in a wild clown suit virtually put him over the edge; when Truman saw this hideous apparition coming at him, with its giant red nose and flaming orange hair, he began to tremble so violently that I thought I was going to have to sweep bits and pieces of chihuahua up off the floor.

"He's not his usual lovey-dovey self," I explained to the disappointed clown. "He's never seen anyone in costume before."

The clown sniffed. "That's the way I usually get treated when I'm *not* in costume!"

When Truman turned his nose up at the ham and cheese at the buffet table, I knew I'd made a big boo-boo. It's one thing to dress your dog up; it's another to subject him to a nervous breakdown. I promptly whisked the beleaguered animal off, far away from the madding crowd and into one of the bedrooms, where I came upon another fugitive partygoer, who was nursing her eight-month-old daughter. We exchanged tales of new motherhood, which I'm not sure she appreciated as much as I did, especially when Truman jumped out of my arms, ran around inspecting the room, and started to lift his leg right by her foot.

"Hey!" I yelled, grabbing him.

"Oh, well," she said, smiling graciously. "It's still a lot better than changing diapers."

I took Truman out for a walk. He was restless and insecure in the strange neighborhood, and I wondered why the hell I'd ever brought him in the first place.

But God knew. When I returned, I went in search of Steven, to suggest that since it was after midnight, it might be time to bid our adieus. I wandered out onto the back patio. Except for the flickering candles on the tables it was pitch black, and I couldn't see anything or anyone very clearly. Some vague shape called out, "What's your dog's name?"

"Truman," I replied, steeling myself for the inevitable next question at a gay gathering.

"Oh, how cute. After Truman Cap—"

"No!" I cut him off. "After *Harry* Truman."

And then my prayer of a lifetime was answered, when I heard another voice say, "I knew Harry Truman."

Was I having auditory hallucinations?

"Who said that?" I addressed the darkness.

A friendly-looking older gentleman in a smart tweed suit came into view.

"I did," he said, smiling as he held out his hand.

"You knew Harry Truman? Really?"

"Well, perhaps that's a bit presumptuous," he admitted,

laughing. "We weren't exactly buddies. But I met him a number of times when I was in Independence."

"You must have been awfully young," I said, instantly making a friend for life.

"Aren't you sweet!" he beamed. He told me his name—Albert Peckham—and explained that he was an antiques appraiser at the prestigious Butterfield's, on Sunset Boulevard.

"Let's just say I was a *younger* man! It was around 1965, and I was visiting friends in Kansas City. Every morning I'd walk their dog for them. Well, I'd go over to Independence—across the fence, you know—because another friend of mine, Milton Perry, ran the Truman Library there. I was affected by the Truman mystique, like any tourist. And one morning, as I was walking down the street, along came Harry Truman, who was walking *his* dog. We crossed paths like that a few times and chatted."

"Wow!" I exclaimed. "It must have been like seeing God."

"It was, in a way." Albert laughed. "I'd never met a U.S. president before, and Truman was such a legend. I didn't really know what to do the first time, whether to nod and continue on my way or what. I didn't want to intrude upon his morning walk; I figured people bothered him enough. So I just smiled and said, 'Good morning, Mr. President.' And he stopped and gave me a big smile, and shook my hand, and said, 'That's a nice dog you have there. What's his name?' And before I knew it, we'd started chatting."

"That sounds just like Harry," I said.

"Oh, he was the most disarming man. Completely unaffected. I'd heard that over and over about him, and it was absolutely true. He was so charming and so nice—and he certainly didn't *have* to be."

I nodded. "Well, you know, he once said, 'Courtesy is the cheapest thing in the world. It's a wonder people don't make more use of it.'"

"Oh, yes, that was him to a T," Albert agreed. "I really think he simply loved to meet people. Milton Perry—my friend who ran the Truman Library, who had been Truman's personal secretary for many years—told me that if Harry happened upon a stranger or a tourist during one of his walks, he'd go right over to him and hold out his hand and say, 'How do you do. Welcome to Independence. I'm Harry Truman.' As if you didn't know! Milton also said that often Harry would pop into the Truman Library unannounced and give any visitors who were there a personal guided tour! He was that unpretentious."

"He never was impressed by himself," I said. "Which is one of the nicest compliments you can pay anyone, I think. I loved what he said about the office of the presidency: 'You see, the thing you have to remember is when you get to be President there are all those things, the twenty-one-gun salutes, all those things, and you have to remember it isn't for you. It's for the presidency, and you've got to keep yourself separate from that in your mind.'"

"My, you certainly know a lot about him," said Albert admiringly.

"Well, I'm writing a book about him."

"A book?" He was impressed. "Really?"

"Sort of." I told Albert about how both Harry Truman and Truman the dog had been my rod and staff during my difficult journey through the valley of the shadow of death.

"What a wonderful tribute," he said, "to *everyone*. Harry Truman, your husband, dogs—and yourself."

"Me?"

A Widow, a Chihuahua, and Harry Truman

"Certainly. You've obviously got a lot of pluck, to write a book like that. I think Harry Truman would have been proud of you."

"I never thought of it that way. I just thought maybe he'd be proud to be remembered this way."

"I'm sure it would have tickled him no end."

"Can you tell me what he looked like? If there was anything about him that stood out to you?"

"Well, I remember he was about average height, maybe a little taller than I. I honestly don't remember much about the way he looked, although that dazzling smile—he still had it. A wonderful, wonderful smile."

"Anything else?" I pressed Albert, as though every one of his words were a glimmering pearl I was trying to catch in my hand before it disappeared forever into the darkness.

"Oh, my, it was so long ago. I wish I'd written down my impressions. Well, he was such a *Missourian*, you know? I remember being struck by that right off."

"What, exactly, is a Missourian?"

"Oh, a Missourian is always very up-front. Missourians say what's on their mind and don't beat about the bush. Truman had what I call a 'midwestern mind.' A no-nonsense mind. His attitude was, Everything is the way it should be and it's all in its proper perspective. To give you an example, I'd run into him and he'd say, 'Well, it's gonna be a cold winter.' And I'd say, 'How do you know?' And he'd say, 'Because I can feel it in my bones.' And I remember thinking, isn't that just like a Missourian. This is the way it is because this is the way it's always been and this is the way it always will be.

"Oh, my," he exclaimed, looking at his watch. "It's almost 1:00 A.M.! Time for me to be toddling off. Lovely meeting you." He held out his hand, Harry Truman style. "And best of luck with your book."

"Let me ask you one more thing, Albert," I said. "Would you say Harry Truman was an American first, or a Missourian first?"

He laughed. "That's a very good question. But I'd have to say, definitely a Missourian. Such a product of his past. He was always very close to his roots; he never really wanted to be anywhere but in Independence. That's not to say that he wasn't the most loyal American in the world. But I think that to a Missourian, Missouri and America are one and the same. We coastal people are foreigners!"

"Say goodbye to Albert," I said to Truman, holding out his paw for Albert to shake. "There. Now you've touched a man who touched the man you were named after. This is a big moment, Truman; I hope you won't forget it."

Truman looked up at me beseechingly, as if to say, "I won't. Now can we go home?"

I'll always be indebted to Albert Peckham, whose wonderful reminiscences made me feel as if I myself were suddenly back on the quiet, courtly streets of Independence, Missouri, chatting with the man I most admired in the whole wide world. I could feel the nip in the fall air, and the warmth of Harry Truman's hand, and I could hear him say, "That's a nice little dog you have there. What's his name?"

And when I answered, "Truman," I'll bet he wouldn't have said, "After Truman Capote?"

Chapter 23

A Turning Point

Everybody is headed for the same place,
and they are headed on the same train, and
under the same engineer.

There comes a time in the grieving process when you throw in the towel and stop trying to fight reality. A time when you're so damn exhausted from waging a war that was lost from the start that you're finally ready to cry uncle and say, "Okay, he's dead and he's not coming back, and I've got to make my way now without him."

The loss experts classify this turning point as "acceptance," and it's supposed to be the final stage of grief. But I don't know if we ever learn to really *accept* the death of a loved one. *Acclimation* might be a better word—acclimation to the inevitable, to a fate we're powerless to alter. And as for a *final* stage of grief—well, I have my doubts about that one too. You'll always miss the person; there will always be moments for the rest of your life when you mourn not only his or her loss but the loss of what might have been.

I found, with Adam's death, that I had not just one but many losses to face. One particularly painful loss was that of the chance to know him on the deeper level that comes with the years. I was really just beginning to discover the wealth of wonderful things about this complex, quiet man, and I often think of all the things about him that I never got to know. And I think of the future we never got to have—the things we never got to do, the special closeness of long-married life that we never got to experience.

There was the loss of my identity as Adam's wife. Although I'd had a career and a life of my own for too many years to define myself through Adam, our marriage had made us a unit, a partnership. Don't get me wrong; I'm a great believer in the many virtues of being single and free. But I also loved being married, having that special person to share and grow with. After Adam's death I felt empty, bereft, as though half of me had been amputated. I had to redefine who I was, and what my purpose was, once Adam was gone.

And there was the loss of lovemaking. Not just sex, but the physical expression of love that takes so many forms, both passionate and peaceful. As Adam grew sicker and more frail, our sex life naturally dwindled. But our love life never did. There were still the cuddles, the kisses, the endearments. As he faded away from me, bit by bit, I would hold his hand and wonder how in the name of God I was going to live without his touch, without the security of knowing he was always there to reach out to.

These are losses I *still* mourn. But about a year after I moved away from Santa Paula, I had an epiphany of sorts: I realized,

A Widow, a Chihuahua, and Harry Truman

one lovely night when spring was just surrendering to summer and the air was so soft it felt like Adam's light touch on my cheek, that I had come to view my husband's death as one of those aspects of a greater scheme whose wisdom belongs to God and not us.

This moment of enlightenment occurred during one of my midnight walks with Truman and the cats. Not being a walker by nature, I at first found it hard to muster up the energy to take Truman out three or four times a day. Our street is on a steep hill, and there's no getting around it; you either start off up the hill to the left or down the hill to the right, but either way you have to make that arduous upward climb.

There are about twenty acres of undeveloped land across from my house, and when you turn right at the top of the hill you find yourself on a genuine country road leading into the wild. It's as though L.A. had suddenly vanished into the mist. My twin brother lives in rural Michigan, on twenty-two acres, and when I visit him I love to steal out and take middle-of-the-night strolls through the woods. So whenever I turn onto the road at the top of my hill, I feel like I'm back in Michigan. It's a very appealing sensation, because I can rev my imagination up and pretend that the normal boundaries of time and space have dissolved and I'm really, finally, in the Twilight Zone.

On this night that I'm recalling—the night of my epiphany—the full moon was out and the road seemed painted with silver. Truman danced in front of me, Petie and Rhonda marched beside me, and all of God's creatures seemed to be having their own private party. A mother rabbit and her babies cavorted in front of a bush, flying into the air and disappearing when Truman lunged at them. A big old possum waddled down the path, eyes glittering like the stars. The cries of the coyotes echoed from the canyon below.

I plopped down on some grass, breathed deeply, and let myself feel a part of the glorious spring night. It was so quiet that I could hear nature talking, and the many wonderful scents of spring—hyacinth, orange blossom, night-blooming jasmine—were intoxicating. I played a game, pretending that I was a blade of grass, a tree, a rabbit, a star. I listened to the mysterious world we never hear in the deafening mad rush of the day. Truman came bounding over into my lap and the cats surrounded me, rubbing up against me and purring. And suddenly I realized that for the first time since Adam's death, I wasn't wishing that he was there beside me. Not that I wouldn't have *wanted* him to be there, but I didn't *need* him there to feel at peace with the moment, at one with myself.

As I sat there on the moonlit grass, I thought about Adam's death. What did it really mean? I watched a baby rabbit poke its head out of a bush. That rabbit might live for a few years or it might die this night, in the jaws of a coyote or a cat. Its lifespan was up for grabs, but one thing was certain: sooner or later it *would* die. I stroked Truman; he would die too, someday, and so would Petie and Rhonda and so would I. There was absolutely nothing I could do about this; it was the natural law.

So, if Adam had to die, as every living thing does, did it really matter when? Would it have been any easier twenty years from now? Sure, I would have had twenty extra years to know and enjoy him. But wouldn't it have been even harder, in a way, to let go after all that time? I thought of the grieving group I'd attended at our local hospice after Adam had died. There were widows younger than I, whose husbands had died in their thirties of cancer and who were left with small children.

A Widow, a Chihuahua, and Harry Truman

There were widows my age, whose husbands had dropped dead of heart attacks or been killed in accidents. There were old widows, whose husbands had died after fifty years of marriage. And not one of them said that it was any easier, having your husband die after five years or after fifty, or having him die suddenly instead of wasting away. I saw then that while some deaths are better than others for the person who dies, there is no "good" death for the survivors. So it really doesn't matter how or when death comes to you.

There's an amazing story by Mark Twain called "The Mysterious Stranger." Twain was one of the world's greatest humorists, of course, but this story is anything but a rib-tickler. In fact, it's Twain at his most darkly philosophical. The story takes place in medieval times; a stranger, handsome and charming, comes to a village and immediately endears himself to all the children. He has magical powers and can perform all sorts of wondrous feats. In addition, he's wise beyond wise. But when the children ask him his name, he replies, "Satan."

The children soon learn that Satan knows everyone's allotted lifespan, and that he has the power to change that span for any individual. When Satan tells the youngsters that he is going to engineer the deaths of two of their little friends, they're distraught and beg him to desist. Satan replies that if he does not intervene, one will be destined for a life as a paralyzed cripple and the other for years of pain ending in the committing of a crime and subsequent execution. "Am I not kind?" he asks. In other words, aren't there worse fates than death?

Mark Twain lost his own beloved daughter when she was quite young. This story grew out of his own struggle with grief, his own attempt to put death in some sort of perspective that would allow him to live with it. And now, as I sat on the grass along my country road in the middle of the night, feeling no more and no less than an infinitesimal part of nature, I was able to admit that death might indeed have been not Adam's enemy but his best friend. He'd had several small strokes before his cancer was diagnosed, and the doctor had warned us that these might be precursors to a bigger one somewhere down the line. What if he'd survived his cancer, only to be crippled for the rest of his life by a massive stroke? What if he'd been paralyzed, unable to speak, unable to do anything for himself? What would that have done to him, to his sense of dignity and manhood? What if I'd had to care for an invalid for the better part of my life? What would that have done to me? Perhaps death had been my best friend too, allowing me to go on with my life, to discover a new destiny—to write this book.

As I thought about all these things, my animals seemed to appreciate the profundity of the moment. Petie gave me his most intent, piercing look, the one that would cause Adam to comment, "That cat knows everything we're thinking." Rhonda blinked and butted her head against my leg. And Truman cocked his head and stared straight into my eyes, as if to say, "I don't know what you're thinking but I know you're feeling better, and that's all *I* care about."

When we started for home, I realized something else. Over time, the hill had become considerably easier for me to traverse. In the beginning I had dreaded the imposing climb and the physical discomfort that went along with it. But months of walking it had obviously paid off; my muscles were stronger, my heart in better shape. I didn't get winded like I used to; I was no longer afraid of the journey.

A Widow, a Chihuahua, and Harry Truman

That was a lot like the grieving process. Time was working its magic after all; the mountain of despair I'd faced after Adam died, that back then had seemed far to steep to ever conquer, was now no more intimidating than a country road in the moonlight, a road that led not away from pain but straight back to the self, the source of all true healing.

Chapter 24

Letting Go

When you feel there's something you have to do
and you know in your gut you have to do it, the sooner
you get it over with the better off everybody is.

Adam's ashes were still on the closet shelf.

The second anniversary of his death was approaching, and I was beginning to feel like a fool. Why the hell was I hanging on to them? Why couldn't I grow up and wipe my nose and face the fact that they were just ashes, nothing more than a memory of a presence, not that presence itself?

I was talking to an older widow friend one day when the subject came up.

"Oh, I carted Hank's ashes around in the trunk of the car for a year," she said. "I'd drive up north, to scatter them at his favorite spot by the ocean, and I'd end up not being able to do it and I'd drive home. I just wasn't ready."

"What finally happened?" I asked.

"Well, one day I was getting something out of the trunk

and Hank was in the way, and I said to him, 'Move over!' And suddenly I thought, Oh, hell, it's time to get rid of him. And I did. I scattered the ashes at the sea and released him, and that was that. Believe me, when you finally do it, you can't believe how much lighter you feel."

Lighter? It seemed to me my heart would be terribly heavy at the second parting.

"Oh, no, it wasn't like that," she said. "I felt lighter. I don't know, like laughing."

Well, when I thought of Adam's cremains, I didn't feel like laughing. The very idea of going to our special place—the hotel in San Luis Obispo—and scattering them in the stream by the old mill made me cringe. *Laughing?* At the place where you'd had your honeymoon? The place where you'd made love and rejoiced in each other and thought that life together was just beginning, when in reality it was almost over? To go back to that place, with the husband you adored now in a small black box, nothing more than a pile of ash that would slip right through your fingers if you tried to hold it? Oh, yeah. It was a real riot.

And then something completely unexpected happened.

I went to see the movie *Smoke Signals*. There was a big buzz going around about this low-budget independent feature, shot on location at a reservation in Idaho and using a primarily Native American cast. It was about the love-hate relationship between a young boy, Victor, and his father, Arnold Joseph, an alcoholic by turns kind and cruel, who one day gets into his beat-up pickup truck and disappears, never to return.

Victor grows up fatherless and hurting. He has a friend, Thomas, whose parents had died in a terrible fire on the reservation when he was an infant. They, too, have a love-hate relationship, feuding and fussing, never able to see eye to eye on anything.

One day Victor's mother receives a phone call from a strange woman in Arizona, who identifies herself as the neighbor of Arnold Joseph, who has just died. She has his ashes. Would someone like to come for them?

So Victor Joseph, now a big, strapping, handsome twenty-one-year-old, and Thomas set out on the Greyhound bus (shades of *A Trip to Bountiful*) to make the painful journey to pick up Arnold Joseph's remains.

I won't go into the whole story, which is incredibly beautiful. But at the end, when Victor Joseph releases his father's ashes to the wind and the river, and howls with pain like a wolf and dances with joy like the jumping salmon, I was a basket case. The tears streamed down my cheeks and I thought, "I've got to do it. I've got to let Adam go."

Then the credits came on and I noticed the names of the two actors who'd played Victor and Thomas: Adam Beach and Evan Adams.

Two Adams. I got a chill.

A couple of weeks later I saw the movie again. At the final scene, where Arnold Joseph's ashes fly into the wind as though swept up into a lover's arms, I shook with sobs again. Then I went home and called the hotel in San Luis Obispo and made a reservation for the following Friday—the second anniversary of Adam's death.

"That's for this Friday, leaving Saturday, correct?" said the young man at the desk.

"Correct."

"Okay. Now I'll give you your confirmation number, which will be my name."

A Widow, a Chihuahua, and Harry Truman

"Your name? I've never gotten a name for a confirmation number before."

"Well, that's how we do it now."

"What's your name?" I asked.

"Adam," he replied.

I froze.

"Are you still there?" he asked.

"Uh, yeah. Yeah, I'm here," I whispered.

"Remember, now. Your confirmation number is 'Adam.'"

"Oh, I'll remember," I said, and hung up, knowing for sure now that I was doing the right thing. After all, I'd just received confirmation from Adam.

That Friday I took Truman to Sant Kaur's and embarked on my own journey of healing.

When I got to the hotel and unpacked, I realized that there were some logistical problems to be solved. First of all, I couldn't dump all of the ashes into the old mill stream. There was too much of them, and there were some large chunks of bone besides. So I'd have to set aside a symbolic sample for this particular mission and figure out what to do with the rest of them.

Second, it was illegal to scatter human cremains in a public place. If I'd wanted to be a law-abiding citizen, I would have gotten the Neptune Society to scatter them at sea, or Adam's old pal down by the airport, Chuck Sisto, to scatter them from his plane over Santa Paula. But this was something I felt I had to do alone, at a very private place, a place dear to Adam's heart. Which meant that I had to do it late at night, when there was no one else around.

The evening passed slowly. I wondered how, exactly, I should structure my little ceremony, what I should say and do. Even though, theoretically, it would be just me standing there alone at the old mill, we all know it wouldn't be. Adam would be there, along with God knows how many other spirits, and I felt the sacredness of the event. I thought of *Smoke Signals*, and how natural a part of life ritual is to Native American culture. Victor Joseph's mother, standing at the door of her dilapidated old house, closing her eyes and raising the coffee can with her husband's ashes inside high above her head in silent communion with the Great Spirit. Victor Joseph, doing a ritual dance in jeans and an open shirt. Thomas, closing his eyes and spinning tales at the drop of a hat in the great storyteller tradition.

But in Western culture, we're awkward with ritual. It tends to make us feel silly, embarrassed. What if somebody were to see me, dropping Adam's ashes into the stream and saying a prayer or singing with the wind? They'd probably call the cops on me, or at least hotel security.

At 2:00 A.M. I put on my jacket, pocketed the pretty glass bottle that held a small portion of the ashes, and stole quietly out of my room. Feeling like a prowler on the grounds, constantly glancing around me to make sure no one was watching, I went out to the old mill.

The big waterwheel turned round and round in the stream, slowly, making a soft, splashing sound that was comforting in its steady rhythm. It was a warm night, just like the night Adam had died, and the air was fragrant with honeysuckle and night-blooming jasmine. Except for the chirping of the crickets and the croaking of a few frogs, it was very, very quiet. There wasn't another soul around. Not a living one, anyway.

I took the little glass bottle out of my jacket pocket. Then I started talking to Adam.

"Honey," I said. "I'm back at our favorite place. I know

you led me here, and I know you're right here with me. I know you felt it was time for me to release your ashes, in order to set us both free."

Then I began to cry. "I miss you so," I whispered. "Right now, right here, I miss your hand in mind. We were always holding hands, always touching, remember? People used to watch us and smile. You loved that; you used to say, 'I think it makes people happy, to see two eejits in love, don't you?'"

I went on like that for awhile, recounting the magical, precious things about our love. One by one I released them, like stones dropped into the water.

Then I said, "I wish you hadn't had to die so soon. I wish you hadn't had to suffer so much. But most of all, I wish you peace. I pray that you're happy now, and busy, and surrounded by flowers, like Andrea said, and angels too. Lots and lots of angels, who'll watch out for you until I get there and can take care of you again, forever."

I emptied the bottle into the water and watched the ashes as they floated away and disappeared.

I didn't feel like laughing. But I *was* beginning to feel lighter.

The next day I drove up to the hill where Adam had so loved to take me, overlooking Santa Paula. Because the local hospital had been built there, it was known by the decidedly unromantic name of "Hospital Hill." But it had been a romantic place to us. We'd stand there, taking in the stunning view of the mountains and valley, Adam pointing out the barely discernible roof of our house far in the distance. Or we'd go up at night to look at the stars and watch the twinkling lights of the city below.

I thought of the day Adam had gone to the hospital for some awful treatment or other and we'd walked out slowly, he shuffling along with his walker and attached to an oxygen tank. I asked him if he'd like to stop and look at the view, and he said yes. It was a beautiful day, sunny and warm, and as we stood there looking out at the mountains and the valley and the houses, everything seemed unreal, as though the world were fading away before my eyes. I put my arm around Adam; he felt so small, so fragile, not at all like the sturdy fellow who'd first taken me up that hill.

He put a thin arm around me.

"Thank you," he said.

"For what, honey?"

"For taking the time to stop here. It means so much, you know."

That was Adam. Grateful for the least little thing.

As we stood there a few minutes more, I knew that *he* knew that it was the last time he would ever gaze out at his beloved view, from his beloved hill. I thought that he must feel like Moses, looking out at the Promised Land, knowing that he would never live to reach it, saying goodbye even as he was saying hello.

But he was back here now. I took the black box with the rest of his ashes out of the trunk. Then I went over to the tree that we used to sit under. There was a strong breeze, and when I took a handful of the ashes and threw them into the air, they came back at me, covering me in a fine dust.

I threw handful after handful into the wind. As the ashes swirled around me, everything seemed to be covered with Adam—the leaves, the ground, the rocks. He was part of the hill now. He was the earth, the wind, the trees. I felt him everywhere, but most of all I felt him in my heart. Scattering his ashes hadn't meant losing him. Rather, I felt even closer to him, as though I were saying hello even as I said goodbye.

I kept a final portion of the ashes to scatter with Angel's at another of our favorite places up in Marin County. This I did some months later, releasing both man and cat to the wind, which made no distinction between them. After all, ashes, like souls, are equal before God.

Chapter 25

Now We Are Three

It's impossible for a man to be President of the
United States without learning something.

To paraphrase Harry Truman, it's impossible for a human being to go through a loss without learning something.

In my case, I learned all sorts of things. Who I was (somebody stronger than I'd thought). What I still had to live for (a hell of a lot). That time *is* a miracle cure after all.

But most important, I learned how to throw a dog party.

When Truman turned three, I decided that it was time for a birthday celebration. I figured it would be simple: a few dogs, some party hats, a cake for the grownups, and treats for the four-leggeds. Of course, in my pre-Truman life, I would have relegated such excesses to the category of extreme stupidity. But since my conversion to the Church of the Mad Dog Owner, I seemed to have lost all sense of sociopolitical proportion.

I made out the guest list: his girlfriend, Missy; his best pal, Buddy; old Geraldine from down the street—his social circle *was* a little on the small side. But I consoled myself with the fact that in the realm of friendship it's quality, not quantity, that counts.

The next item on the agenda was party hats.

These wouldn't be a problem for Missy and Geraldine, whose heads were about the size of a small child's. But as far as I knew, party hats for pinheads weren't exactly hot commercial properties.

I called Joanna, a dog-party veteran.

"I used to make Buddy's hats out of those cone things that go in ice-cream dishes," she said. "I got them from a restaurant-supply store near where I lived then. I don't know where you could find them around your area, but we'll think of something."

I found the answer at the drugstore, in the party section. Party paper cups! All I had to do was turn them upside down, punch a couple of holes in them, and tie them under chihuahua chins with color-coordinated streamers. I might have a career yet in the doggie design industry.

The big day was almost upon us when, alas, the cancellations began to arrive.

Something came up for Sant Kaur that weekend and Missy had to regretfully decline. Old Geraldine was having a spell, and May didn't think it would be a good idea to subject her to the rowdy goings-on of the younger set.

That left Buddy.

"Bring Truman on over," said Joanna. "We'll have the party here and Todd can take pictures."

I arrived with the birthday boy and the cupcakes, candles, and cups. Buddy was already barking hysterically at the window when we pulled up, and Truman was so excited that he shot out the car door like greased chihuahua lightning, wailing with joy.

Although Truman and Buddy have had a million play dates, Joanna and I never cease to be enchanted by their ritual greeting. Truman flies through the door and he and Buddy dance around each other in circles, grinning from ear to ear. Then they tear around the house, making a deafening clatter on the hardwood floors—a sound that I refer to as the thundering hooves of the chihuahua cavalry. Finally they race out into the backyard, where they frolic for about ten or fifteen minutes, tearing inside again to jump up on their mommies' laps for kisses. Then they gallop out again.

As Todd loaded the camera, Joanna handed me a hole-puncher and I made the party hats. We set the table—she graciously offered her best lace tablecloth for the occasion—and put out a cupcake for both Buddy and Truman (whose cupcake had a numeral-three candle on top). Then we dragged the dogs in for "their" party. We tied their hats on, lit the candle, and sang "Happy Birthday" while Todd snapped away.

I wish that I could say the whole thing had been more eventful, but that was about it. After we'd taken the boys' pictures, Joanna, Todd, and I sat around the table eating their cupcakes while they ran around the room sniffing each other's behinds. Then they lay down, nicely and quietly, on the couch.

"Truman's been so good lately," I said to Joanna. "He doesn't run out the door anymore—in fact, he stands there, waiting for me to give the signal that it's okay to go out. I don't have to keep him on the leash; he follows me just like a real dog. And he *listens* to me. If I say no, he backs off. If I say, 'Come here,' he runs over to me. I don't know how the hell it happened."

A Widow, a Chihuahua, and Harry Truman

"He's grown up," Joanna explained. "He's not a puppy anymore. He's matured."

Suddenly I realized that the day I'd never thought would come was here. Truman had actually become a Good Dog.

I developed the pictures the next day. As I looked through them, I couldn't believe that Truman was three already. Where had the years gone?

I thought back to those early days of puppyhood. The chunks gnawed out of the table legs, the "presents" on the floor, the ubiquitous treasure pile that seemed to swallow up all my possessions, one by one, like a black hole. I thought of the day Truman had chewed off the cap to my blood-pressure meds and I'd found pills strewn all over the floor, counting them hastily, hands shaking, praying that he hadn't swallowed any. I thought of the countless times he'd run off and almost gotten killed, and the times I'd despaired of ever being able to take him places and not worry about whether or not he'd destroy a rug (and a friendship along with it). How, I wondered, had both of us lived through it?

Then I thought of where *I'd* been nearly three years earlier. Grieving, despondent, half the time not wanting to live, unable for the life of me to believe that I'd ever know the sensation of happiness again.

I thought of Santa Paula, with all its bittersweet memories. And I suddenly remembered a song I'd written, way back then, shortly after Adam had died and before I'd gotten Truman, when I'd so dreaded going home to that lonely, empty house.

I'd called it "No One to Come Home to Anymore." I can remember only a bit of it now, because I've since lost it (probably mercifully), but it was inspired by all the corny country music that I, who'd been trained to be a concert pianist, never would have dreamed of listening to ordinarily but suddenly found so comforting in the midst of grief. All those country songs are about losing the one you love, either to someone else or to death, and they're not necessarily limited to lovers. Mothers and fathers, grammas and grampas, dogs and hogs— you name it, they all come in for syrupy eulogies, and you realize just how universal love and loss are, and how true it is that misery loves company.

Anyway, my song went something like this:

There's no one to come home to anymore
Nobody to greet me at the door
Nobody to kiss
Nobody to miss
No one to come home to anymore

There's nobody to sit with by the fire
Nobody to kindle my desire
Nobody to care
Whether or not I'm there
No one to come home to anymore

The house sits there so empty and so cold
There's nobody to hold me and to hold
No matter how I pray
I can't go on this way
With no one to come home to anymore

I began to smile then as I thought of how, when I come home these days, a little dog is dancing wildly at the door, whimpering with joy and shooting three feet in the air like a

Mexican jumping bean. How everything has to stop while I sit down and kiss him and let him work off his excitement by biting my nose and licking my face.

As I looked at the pictures of Truman with his Happy Birthday paper-cup party hat sitting askew atop his head, his cupcake with the lighted candle, and his idiot mom holding him up proudly for the camera, I remembered a story that Margaret Truman told in her biography of her dad, *Harry S. Truman*, about something that had happened when her little boy was just my Truman's age.

Three-year-old Clifton had a hobby horse which he was very fond of riding too vigorously. One morning at breakfast the horse tipped over and Kif, as we call him, went sprawling. Mother and the nurse both jumped up and rushed toward him. The sight of this feminine consolation immediately started him whimpering.

Dad took charge. "Leave him alone," he said. Then in a very ungrandfatherly voice he said, "Get up. Pick up the horse and get back on." Kif was so startled, he forgot all about crying and obeyed the presidential order. It was a pretty big and heavy hobbyhorse, but he rolled it over and got back on.

I thought that Harry Truman would probably be snorting in he-man disgust at the sight of two foolish women making a silly birthday party for two damn dogs. But then I thought that he might just give me an approving nod at how I'd managed, in these last three rocky years, to pick myself up off the ground, get back up on the hobbyhorse, and build myself a new life.

Oh, I'm not saying I don't still have down days. But thank God they're much fewer and farther between. Of course, I still miss Adam. But it isn't the kind of missing it was three years ago. The pain of loss is no longer excruciating; while the scar tissue is still tender, the wound has healed over. I still cry, from time to time, when I think of him. But more often I laugh at the memory of the fun we had together, which is just the way he'd want it.

I imagine he might be chuckling right now, as a matter of fact, at the irony that his replacement came in the form of a nasty, yippy little tweeter. But that's the punchline of the big joke the cosmos likes to play on us from time to time, to cut us down to size. We humans think we're so far above animals, when in reality it's downright humiliating how much we can learn from them about selflessness, protecting and nourishing the young, loyalty, and other qualities that too few two-leggeds possess.

My life changed for the better when I began looking at my cats and my dog not as mere pets but as sentient beings just like me. I developed an interesting exercise, in which I would study them carefully, noting all the things we had in common. Two ears, two eyes, a nose, teeth, a tongue, a chin, an under-the-chin, armpits, wrists, and elbows. In fact, the only things that seemed to separate me physically from my animals were a tail and fur. And our most basic needs were the same: food, shelter, and love.

I was grateful for the loyalty of Truman and the cats—the way they'd lie in bed with me for days on end when I had the flu, or curl up beside me when I was crying. There are a hell of a lot of humans who won't be there for you when you need them, but I have yet to meet an animal that, if you give it love, won't remain right there by your side through thick and thin.

I admired them for abilities I could never hope to possess. I would watch in awe as Petie jumped lightly and delicately onto a shelf of objets d'art eight feet above the ground, never so much as rattling a single one of the pieces, a feat that would have taken a gymnast years to perfect but that he performed with the utter nonchalance of instinct. I marveled at Truman's uncanny ability to sense things before they were going to happen, or hear things miles away. I learned to appreciate the animals not as my property but as separate but equal beings, from whose wisdom I could learn much if I was willing to watch and listen.

Yes, love comes in many shapes, sizes, and forms, some human, some divine, some feline, some canine. And whatever shape it takes, it always has something magical to teach us, about ourselves and about the gift of life we too often take for granted.

When Adam died, I no longer saw life as a gift; instead, rudely and abruptly, it had become a burden. But Truman the dog helped me to reclaim the sense of joy and aliveness I'd feared I'd lost forever. By making me laugh, he helped me to put things in their proper perspective. By forcing me to tend to him, he drew me out of myself. By loving me unconditionally, with his entire little heart and soul, he opened my own heart and soul.

Although I never thought I'd be able to say the words, I *am* happy once more. I have my good, close friends, my writing, a life full of surprises to look forward to. I have a sense of place, and a sense of purpose.

And I have somebody now to come home to. Somebody to greet me at the door, to kiss and to miss, to hold me and to hold. To cherish and protect, in sickness and in health, till death do us part.

I have, at last, found love—and life—again.